£ 6.50
two

9/32

REGIONAL ARCHAEOLOGIES **NORTH WALES**

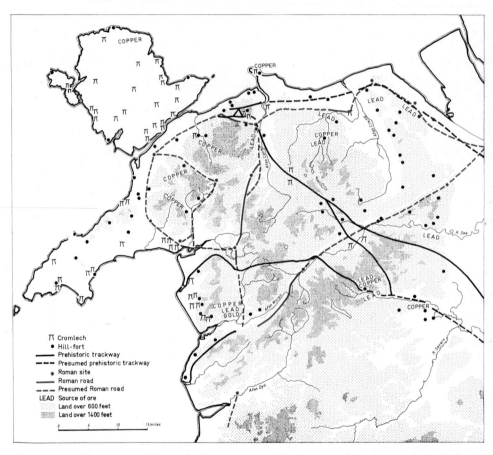

Frontispiece *Map of North Wales showing main monuments and trackways in relation to physical features and mineral deposits*

REGIONAL ARCHAEOLOGIES

North Wales

BY KATHERINE WATSON

CORY, ADAMS & MACKAY

Regional Archaeologies

GENERAL EDITOR: D. M. WILSON, M.A., F.S.A.
Reader in Archaeology of the Anglo-Saxon Period at the University of London ;
President of the British Archaeological Association

CONSULTANT EDITOR: A. D. ATIENZA, B.A. (Hons)
Deputy Head Teacher, Whitley Abbey Comprehensive School, Coventry

NORTH WALES

© Katherine Watson 1965

The text is set in 'Monotype' Ehrhardt

First published 1965 by Cory, Adams & Mackay Ltd, 39 Sloane Street, London, SW1

Printed and bound in England by W. & J. Mackay & Co Ltd, Chatham, Kent

Contents

1 MOUNTAINS AND MAN *page* 9

2 AFTER THE ICE AGE 13

3 THE NEOLITHIC PERIOD 15

4 THE BEAKER PEOPLE 27

5 THE BRONZE AGE 31

6 TRACKWAYS, PORTS AND TRADE ROUTES 46

7 THE IRON AGE 52

8 THE ROMANS 65

GAZETTEER OF SITES 73

MUSEUMS 88

READING LIST 88

List of Illustrations

	Map showing monuments and routes	*Frontispiece*
Fig. 1	Time Chart	*page* 8
Fig. 2	Mousterian tool from Pont Newydd	11
Fig. 3	Upper Palaeolithic and Mesolithic flint work	12
Fig. 4	Western Chamber at Dyffryn	16
Fig. 5	Plans of Chamber tombs	17
Fig. 6	Objects from Bryn yr Hen Bobl	18
Fig. 7	The ancestry of passage grave art	21
Fig. 8	Bryn Celli Ddu	22
Fig. 9	Graig Lwyd axes	24
Fig. 10	Map of find places of Graig Lwyd axes	26
Fig. 11	Beakers	28
Fig. 12	Beaker cist	30
Fig. 13	Brymbo beaker	30
Fig. 14	Bronze Age flint work	31
Fig. 15	Corwen mace head	32
Fig. 16	Bronze implements from Ty'n y Pwll	32
Fig. 17	Moulds for axes	33
Fig. 18	Food Vessel from Ty'n y Pwll	34
Fig. 19	Bronze Age funerary pottery	35
Fig. 20	Pigmy cups	36
Fig. 21	The development of the bronze axe	37
Fig. 22	Spearheads	38
Fig. 23	The Nannau bucket	38
Fig. 24	The Harlech shield	39
Fig. 25	Some objects from the Guilsfield hoard	40
Fig. 26	Objects from Late Bronze Age hoards	41
Fig. 27	Map of find places of Beakers and Food Vessels	44
Fig. 28	Boat shaped cist near Llandecwyn	44
Fig. 29	Bryn Cader Faner	45
Fig. 30	Bronze Age trackway at Milltir Gerrig	47

Fig. 31   Bronze sickle from Llanuwchllyn   48
Fig. 32   Axe hammer   48
Fig. 33   Swords   49
Fig. 34   Gold lunula   50
Fig. 35   Jet necklace   50
Fig. 36   Mold cape   51
Fig. 37   Caergwrle bowl   51
Fig. 38   Trawsfynydd tankard   54
Fig. 39   Cerrig y Drudion bowl: pattern on the flange   54
Fig. 40   Moel Hiraddug plaque   55
Fig. 41   The Tal y Llyn shield   55
Fig. 42   Tre'r Ceiri   57
Fig. 43   Muriau'r Gwyddelod   59
Fig. 44   Model of Celtic war chariot   62
Fig. 45   Celtic animals   63
Fig. 46   Capel Garmon firedog   64
Fig. 47   Boar from Roman tile   66
Fig. 48   Roman milestone   67
Fig. 49   Plan of Gop cave   83

ACKNOWLEDGEMENTS

Thanks are due to Messrs Idris Ltd for permission to illustrate the Tal y Llyn shield, which with the other finds has been deposited by them in the National Museum of Wales. It is a privilege also to acknowledge the generous help and kindness of many scholars, friends and owners of objects, in particular from Mr L. Alcock, Mr and Mrs H. Armfield, Prof. R. Atkinson, Mr M. Bevan-Evans, Mr C. Burgess, Mr J. Forde-Johnston, Mr C. Gresham, Mr W. E. Griffiths, Prof. W. Grimes, Mr C. Houlder, Mr R. Livens, Mr I. Longworth, Dr C. McBurney, Mr I. Owen, Mr K. Painter, Dr H. N. Savory, Mr G. Sieveking, the Hon. Mrs Vaughan, Mr W. Watson, Mr K. Williams, Mr R. Williams. The drawings have been done by Mrs Eva Wilson.

Date (approximate)	Vegetation	Important sites or finds	Human cultures and periods	Climatic conditions	Climatic or geological period
BC 78,000	ice			arctic	Pleistocene
	tundra				
70,000	parkland			more temperate	
	tundra	Pont Newydd	Mousterian		
60,000	ice			arctic	
50,000					
40,000					
	parkland			temperate	
30,000	ice	Cae Gwyn	Aurignacian		
	parkland	Ffynnon Beuno		arctic	
				more temperate	
20,000	ice			arctic	
		Ffynnon Beuno	Solutrean		
				sub-arctic	
10,000	end of ice age			cold	
	scrub:			sub-arctic	pre-Boreal
	willow, birch				
(Change of time scale)					
	pine			warm and dry	Boreal
	hazel, oak, elm, lime		MESOLITHIC		
6,000					
	alder			warm and damp	Atlantic
5,000		Prestatyn			
4,000		Dyffryn			
3,000					
2,000	(Once a species of tree is established it continues to flourish in suitable places. The table shows roughly when the species is beginning to spread.)	Graig Lwyd Bryn Celli Ddu Gwaenysgor	NEOLITHIC — BEAKERS	warm and dry	Sub-Boreal
		Merddyn Gwyn			
		Druids' Circle			
		Cwm Moch hoard	BRONZE AGE		
1,000					
		Nannau Bucket Parc y Meirch hoard			
500				cool and wet	Sub-Atlantic
	beech hornbeam	Castell Odo Dinorben	IRON AGE		
AD 0		A.D. 61 Llyn Cerrig Bach	A.D. 61 ROMAN OCCUPATION		
		383. Romans leave			
500					
			A.D. 383 DARK AGES		

Fig. 1 Dates, periods and sites

1 Mountains and Man

THE BUILDING OF THE MOUNTAINS

About 300 million years ago the mountains of Snowdon and Cader Idris, and the Harlech Dome between them, were shaped into the forms we know, but they lay deep beneath the surface of the rocks, at the roots of a high mountain range. Eventually rain, sea, ice, wind and frost removed the covering mountains and left the ancient rocks exposed. The pressure that had pushed up the mountains came from the south. It met the resistance of the hard rock of Anglesey and the Padarn ridge, and squeezed the land between into a great fold running north-east to south-west. This is why all the main lines on the map of North Wales, both ranges of hills and river valleys, run in this direction. The movement of the rocks amounted to only a few inches in a century, but it worked with tremendous force. It caused great heat, acting below a thickness of upper deposits several miles deep. What had been mud was turned to slate, producing some of the greatest slate deposits in the world.

During these *millennia* (time counted in thousands of years) plants and animals were evolving, first in the sea, then on land. In the next 100 million years tropical forests grew, later to be compressed by earth movements into coal, such as is found in Flintshire, while in the sea nearby little creatures built up with their shells and secretions a mud which was to become the limestone appearing along the north coast, along the Clwyd valley and in Anglesey. Then about 100 million years ago the whole area lay again under a chalk-forming sea; and when the Alps and Himalayas rose up in the 'Alpine Storm'

between 60 and 30 million years ago, our region also rose as chalkland, and the courses of many of the main rivers were set. The Ffrangcon, Padarn, Llanberis and Llugwy valleys were cut in the direction of the tilt of the land as it then lay, and not along the north-east/south-west fold of the rocks (then lying beneath the chalk, but today exposed). In time the chalk weathered away altogether. The rivers continued to cut their way through the older rocks, creating mountain passes and linking valleys which provide the main communications of our region at the present day.

About 3 million years ago the coastline and mountain relief of Wales had in general reached the pattern we see today, though the final shaping was the work of ice. At the heart of the mountain folds rose the great dome of Snowdon, surrounded by rings of volcanic hills where weaknesses, caused by the stress of the long series of upheavals, had allowed molten rock from below to squirt up towards the surface. In this rock are veins of gold, crystalline quartz, and the ores of copper, lead, zinc and iron. Where it cooled at the right rate the rock itself crystallized into a material particularly suitable for making the tools which man was to invent so many thousands of years later. The existence of this superior stone, and, later, of the metal ores, was to have a considerable effect on human life in our region.

GLACIATIONS

The history of mankind falls wholly into the last million years. During much of this period

North Wales lay under a sheet of ice hundreds of feet thick. The movements of the ice-sheet carved the wide valleys and rugged crags of the present landscape, and dug out the lakes. As the ice melted it left behind the hillocks and blankets of *boulder clay* (clay mixed with boulders and stones) which now cover much of the land, and deposited 'erratics', or boulders carried from far-away rocks, the largest of which stand so dramatically on mountain-sides and valley bottoms.

There have been four main glacial periods, or *glaciations*, separated by millennia of warm, even hot climate, changing so slowly that it could not be noticed in a man's lifetime, but on the geological time-scale changing very swiftly. They have been named after valleys in Germany. The only one which concerns us is the last one, called Würm. Although traces of man are known in England and elsewhere from the earlier *interglacials* (warm spells between the ice ages), in North Wales there is no evidence that man was present until one of the warmer phases of the Würm glaciation.

DATING

The climate varied much throughout this glaciation, and it is no easy matter to tell when a deposit such as gravel, or bones, or shells, was laid down. Thus we cannot date with certainty the remains of this time. Indeed, no dating can be anything but approximate until man invented a calendar and there are written records. Since the war the atomic analysis of carbon (referred to as Carbon 14) has made it possible to date fairly accurately the vegetable deposits of the last 10,000 years. This method is less accurate for remoter periods. A rough chronology, or time-scale, has been built by the examination of clays and sands and their contents, particularly pollen (fig. 1). It provides a useful frame into which we may fit what is known of human prehistory, provided the dates are recognized

as progressively less exact the farther back in time they lie.

THE WÜRM GLACIATION

From 110,000 B.C. until 60,000 B.C. the climate of Europe was mainly temperate, though there are signs that for some 2,000 years around 78,000 B.C. a colder phase made forests dwindle and sent warmth-loving animals such as lion, hippopotamus and elephant southwards from our latitude, to be replaced by the reindeer and mammoth which feed on scrub and arctic tundra vegetation. They returned slowly northwards again as the climate improved, but just before 60,000 B.C. the ice began a new advance from the polar regions. Winters at first tended to be longer, snow lay at a lower level all through the summer, and in due time forests turned to parkland, parkland to scrub and scrub to bare tundra. Ice from the north pressed down the Irish Sea basin in a great glacier, while smaller glaciers from such high places as Snowdon pushed out to meet and join it. Not for some 20,000 years until shortly before 40,000 B.C. did the ice make a general retreat, though its extent must at times have varied and the climate grown temporarily warmer. For the most part, North Wales was completely under ice. The Early Würm is divided from Main Würm by some 10,000 years between 42,000 B.C. and 32,000 B.C., and the Main Würm itself was interrupted by a warmer spell around 25,000 B.C., when parkland is known to have flourished as far north as the Netherlands. From about 18,000 B.C. each advance during the fluctuations of the ice was smaller than the last. The final retreat, reaching to modern times, dates from about 10,000 B.C. The withdrawal of the ice may still be continuing.

THE EARLIEST HUMAN REMAINS

The earliest period of man's history, and by far the longest, is the *palaeolithic*, or the Old

Stone Age. It lasted until the end of the Ice Age, about 10,000 B.C. in our latitude. Man hunted his food, he had not yet learned to farm or breed stock, and he used stone for making cutting tools and weapons.

The earliest human relic in North Wales is a large molar tooth. It was found in the clay with which glacial melt-waters filled Pont Newydd Cave, in Denbighshire. In the same deposit with the tooth were the worn and jumbled bones of rhinoceros, hippopotamus, elephant, bear, bison, reindeer, hyena and other animals now equally foreign to this region. There were also fragments of stone shaped by man, and some finished implements, of shapes suitable for hunting weapons, for cutting meat or skin, or for carving bone. The human tooth identifies its owner as a member of the extinct Neanderthal species. This species of man had a large brain, but one less complex than that of modern man; he also stood less erect. His face and jaws were heavy and his chin receded. But if not handsome, he was far advanced on the path of human evolution, and highly skilled in working flint and other stone for tools and weapons. The tools from Pont Newydd (fig. 2), now in the Museum of Archaeology at Cambridge, are similar to tools used by Neanderthal men in caves in Derbyshire and Coygan Cave in South Wales. They are classified as Mousterian, being made by the same technique of chipping as the large collection of flint implements found piled yards deep at Le Moustier in France. Here under a sheltered crag by the Dordogne river generations of Neanderthal men lived throughout the Early Würm glaciation, dropping their debris as they cooked, ate and made their tools. This rubbish became the floor for the next generation. Sometimes the dead were carefully buried by the hearth, and the rubbish left by the living continued to accumulate over them.

Like the deposits at Le Moustier, all the caves in the Clwyd valley are full of animal remains. We gain the impression that in Wales game was plentiful and men few.

The reason for the sparse population of Wales at this remote period may be that there is very little flint to be found in the region. Flint was the favourite material for making tools in the Old Stone Age. It can easily be shaped to give a strong, sharp cutting edge. Districts rich in flint attracted the densest human settlement. The Pont Newydd Mousterians managed with whatever stone they could find scattered on the ground surface, the debris of glaciers. Some of their tools are of quartzite and other crystalline rocks, some of a hard shale, two are made from glacial pebbles of flint, and several of the limestone of the cave itself, evidently pieces which had split off from the sides or the roof, as frequently happens in caves from the effects of frost. In South Wales the Mousterians inhabiting Coygan Cave also used the rock of their cave for implements. This is not a usual practice, and points to a close connexion between the two groups of people. In Pont Newydd cave the animal bones are of cold-climate and hot-climate species mixed to-

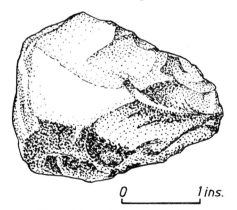

Fig. 2 *Mousterian stone tool from Pont Newydd Cave*

gether. This mixture was caused by flood waters churning together bones which had accumulated in or near the cave over thousands of years of varying climate. Coygan and Paviland caves in South Wales and Cresswell Crag caves in Derbyshire were used regularly by Mousterian hunters of reindeer, mammoth and horse. Thus it seems most probable that at Pont Newydd, too, the Neanderthal hunters occupied the sheltered cave, facing the sun, at a time when the ice-sheets were near, before the climax of the Early Würm glaciation,

at the same period as the other caves were occupied. They would then have looked from the cave mouth on to a treeless expanse of snowy hill-tops and tundra scrub, and lived by hunting the reindeer, bison, horse and cave bear whose bones lay in the cave filling.

HOMO SAPIENS AT TREMERCHION

The next occupation site of North Wales, on the east side of the great Clwyd valley, introduces *Homo sapiens*, the race to which all modern men belong. In the early centuries

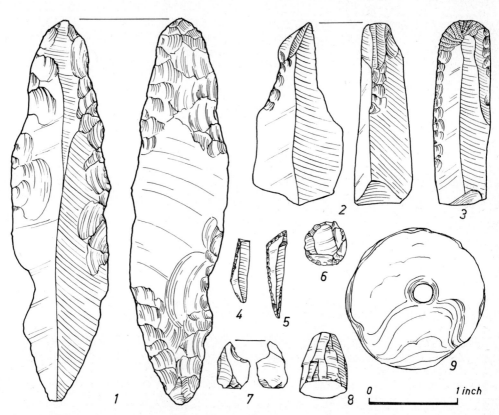

Fig. 3 *Upper Palaeolithic and Mesolithic flint implements.* 1 *Solutrean lance point or knife from Ffynnon Beuno Cave, Tremeirchion,* 2 *Aurignacian graver from Ffynnon Beuno cave,* 3 *Aurignacian end-scraper from Cae Gwyn cave,* 4–9 *chert microliths and core, and pierced oyster shell disc from Prestatyn Mesolithic site.* (1, 2, 3 *after R. E. M. Wheeler 'Prehistoric and Roman Wales'*)

12

of the Main Würm, from about 32,000 B.C. onwards, hunters followed arctic animals westward from eastern Europe. The area round the Dordogne, inhabited earlier by the Mousterians, is also full of Upper Palaeolithic remains from the settlements of the earliest modern men in western Europe. Aurignacian tools (known from Aurignac, in the Dordogne, as the work of these hunters) were found at Cresswell and in South Wales, and also in both Ffynnon Beuno and Cae Gwyn caves, near Tremerchion (fig. 3). These caves lie side by side in the south-facing cliff above a little stream which runs down into the Clwyd.

Most of the pieces are flint tools shaped for scraping and working bone and skin 'scrapers' and 'borers'. They were found under about 15 feet of glacial sands and gravels in the chambers and at the entrance of the caves, together with 1,300 animal teeth (of rhinoceros, hyena, horse and mammoth) and the bones of deer, lion and bear, and sea-shells.

No. 1 in figure 3 is different. It is a lance-point or knife of the type called Solutrean, after a site at Solutré in southern France, with beautiful regular flaking shaping the edge. It was made by a hunter who used the cave about 17,000 B.C.

2 *After the Ice Age*

THE CLIMATE AFTER THE ICE AGE

About 8500 B.C. the British Isles ceased to be a land of perpetual snows. The climate became steadily warmer and trees grew where before there had been only tundra. Birch and willow flourished first and pine followed. Hazel, oak, elm and lime began to spread after 4000 B.C. Beech came last. The mountains, now increasingly covered by forest, were in shape much as we see them today, their shoulders scored and battered by the ice, their lower slopes coated with glacial clay. In the Boreal period, between 6800 B.C. and 5000 B.C., the summers were hotter and the winters colder than now. Between 5000 B.C. and 2000 B.C. the climate was warm, but much wetter. Where the water lay, peat bogs replaced forests, while strong west winds, bringing in rain and mists from the ocean,

prevented forests from growing in exposed places. This is the Atlantic period. The next 1,500 years saw more sunshine again, and this sub-Boreal period, during which human life flourished as never before in our area, allowed people to settle on the higher moorlands, until about 600 B.C. a cold wet phase set in, called the sub-Atlantic, which brought the worst climate that has been known since the end of the glacial period. The table on page 8 gives a list of the climatic phases in relation to the history of man.

As the ice-sheets retreated and vegetation changed, the animal population changed with it. Tundra animals moved northwards, followed by their hunters. Some of the hunters, however, stayed behind and gradually began to move from the caves to open sites in the forests and by the shores, trapping new animals and finding many fish in the warmer waters. This new way of life is known as the *mesolithic* or Middle Stone Age. Little of this can be seen in North Wales, partly because the evidence is probably now under the sea.

CHANGES IN SEA-LEVEL; PEATS AND FORESTS

The water released by the melting of the ice-cap caused the sea-level to rise. But at the same time the land, freed from the weight of ice, also began to rise again, so there was an uneven movement of the shoreline, a movement which has never ceased up to the present. In North Wales there are alternate levels of peat and clay between the tide levels on the coast, showing that the land there was sometimes heathland and sometimes under water. Stumps of trees are bared at low tide in the Dyfi estuary, and in the Menai Straits. Again along the north coast east of Llandudno there are three forest layers below high-tide level. These, and some earlier glacial remains below the high-tide line have inspired the Celtic bards with legends of drowned lands, castles and cities, of Caer Aranrhod and the flooded realm of Gwaelod. As late as Roman times there was land uncovered on the north coast by the ceaseless fluctuation of the sea-level, but even the third layer of forests, whose stumps now emerge so dramatically from the tide, was covered by sea long before men were building cities or even castles.

In early post-glacial times mesolithic people fished and hunted small game in these woods and marshlands. A few of them have left remains far enough inland for them not to be hidden by the sea at the present day. Mesolithic sites are known in North Wales at Aberdaron, Pencilan Head, Newborough Warren, Aberystwyth, Prestatyn and in Gop Cave.

MESOLITHIC SITES IN NORTH WALES

Mesolithic stone work is nearly all very small. At Paviland in South Wales and Cresswell in Derbyshire the continuous reduction of the scale of flint flaking can be followed in the occupation remains, almost from generation to generation. The tools had become very small by the time mesolithic man began to leave his remains in North Wales. At Aberystwyth the mesolithic settlers worked flint pebbles from the shore; at Prestatyn they used the *chert* (a granular flint) found embedded in the limestone rock. Both made microliths: blades and points seldom more than half an inch long, like the latest flint tools found at Paviland or Cresswell. Common shapes were triangles, crescents, points blunted either all down one edge, across the base, or obliquely across one end (fig. 3). These shapes are characteristic of a people who had no axes or adzes to fell trees and work heavy timber, and who avoided heavily wooded territory.

Microliths were mounted, one on each side of a shaft, as the tip of an arrow or dart. They were also set in rows in pieces of wood or bone to make saws, sickles or knives. On rare occasions, though not yet in North Wales, microliths have been found in positions corresponding to the shape of the tool in which they were mounted, or with gum or pitch still on them. These tiny implements are often found in unexpected places; and if they are found in numbers it is important to note how they lie. A wooden or bone handle may have perished, leaving its imprint in the ground, or the stone teeth in place, and this is a much more important find than a pocketful of loose pieces. They often lie near the surface of the ground. In a field between the by-pass road and the town of Prestatyn thousands of microliths have been turned up by the plough. On the cliff above Pared Llechymenyn, Aberdaron, and on Pencilan Head large quantities have been found on the surface. At Aberffraw a Bronze Age burial mound had been built over the ground on which they had been left centuries before, among the shells of nuts eaten by their makers. They occur on the beach at Prestatyn, and scattered in the charcoal found on the floors of Gop Cave.

The flints at Aberystwyth lay with charcoal and burnt stones remaining from fireplaces immediately over the glacial clay (the same formation which sealed up the caves of Ffynnon Beuno and Cae Gwyn), where the Rheidol and Ystwyth rivers join at the foot of a cliff. At Prestatyn a trench dug for a drain revealed a thick layer of charcoal and chert chips and microliths, among which lay a disk of oyster shell with a hole bored in the middle, pieces of sharpened bone, hazelnut shells and the antler tine of a deer. Deer was one of the animals most important to man throughout prehistoric and historic times. Not only did they provide meat, their antler and bone served for implements, and their hide for clothing, tents and rugs, coracles and sails.

From the evidence of sites in Yorkshire, such as the famous Star Carr, and in Scotland, Denmark and elsewhere, we know a little more about the mesolithic people. They used harpoons of bone, fishing-nets, bone or shell hooks, rolled bark floats, amber beads, canoes of tree trunks dug out by burning, and bows. An arrow was lodged in the spine of a man at Téviec in Brittany, and he had been buried with ceremony. In North Wales only two skeletons can be attributed to the Mesolithic period, and these not with certainty.

In northern Europe mesolithic tribes met the challenge of the forest and invented tools for felling trees. They domesticated the dog, learned to make pottery, and bored stone for fitting shafts. How far these advances were the result of the influence of more progressive societies developing round the eastern Mediterranean is not yet certain. In any case this leisurely progress was eventually interrupted by the arrival of new peoples who brought with them revolutionary techniques. *Neolithic* (New Stone Age) culture quickly transformed the land, and the life of all people living on it. The change is justifiably called the neolithic revolution.

3 *The Neolithic Period*

THE FIRST FARMERS, AND A NEW RELIGION

The signs of human life in Mesolithic times are rare and the population must have been extremely small, isolated and savage. Towards the end of the fourth millennium (say 3300 B.C.) great changes occurred. People with herds of cattle (ancestors of the modern small black Welsh mountain cattle), with flocks of sheep, seed corn and probably pigs as well, landed on our shores and began to farm the virgin land. North Wales ceased to be a backwater on the fringes of the inhabited world and became a station on an important trade and migration route which led from the Mediterranean around western Europe to Denmark and the Baltic. The sea henceforth was a highway to Ireland, Brittany, Iberia (the peninsula of Spain and Portugal) and Scotland. All this we know from study of the *cromlechau*, so characteristic of our coastal landscape. These monuments are the ruins of the tombs or temples built by these new-comers, formed of enormous blocks of stone, or *megaliths* (from the Greek *megas*, large, and *lithos*, stone). Eight of these have been excavated in the present century, six on Anglesey, where about twenty-five survive, and at least as many again are recorded but are now completely ruined. This number can be compared with the several hundred which survive in Scotland, over 1,000 in Ireland and perhaps 6,000 in France. Ireland in neo-lithic times was an important religious centre, and Wales lay within its sphere of influence, as indeed it remained until after the decline of the Celtic Church 4,000 years later.

THE CROMLECHAU AT DYFFRYN

The most recently excavated of these neolithic monuments lies behind the school at Dyffryn Ardudwy. It consists of two chambers, one up-slope of the other; the lower, western-most, is the earlier. It is built of five huge stones forming the walls of a chamber 5 feet by 3 feet, a high closing stone across the entrance, and a roofing stone or 'capstone'. The closing stone is set back so that the two side stones, the tallest of the wall stones, form a kind of porch, roofed by the capstone, which, both from the lie of the land and because of the height of the side stones, is tilted upwards at its eastern end. This is a typical *portal dolmen*, well known round the shores of the Irish Sea and common in Ireland. The date of its building is fixed by the contents of a small pit dug in front of the portal. In this pit were large fragments

of five pots, freshly broken before they were put in. They are the same kind of pottery as some that was found 80 miles away across the sea in Pembrokeshire, at Clegyr Boia, on the floor of what had been an oblong house built with wooden posts. It is some of the earliest pottery known in the Irish Sea area, made before 3000 B.C. To each side of the portal a short wall of flat stones fanned out, making a forecourt in which the pit had been dug (fig. 4). All of this had once been covered by an oval cairn (see fig. 5 (*right*)) of stones, only the base of which has remained within living memory. The stones have been used since medieval times at least for building field walls or houses in the village.

Not very long after the building of this cairn the second, larger, cromlech was built

Fig. 4 *The western chamber at Dyffryn seen from the south-east. The wall marks out the forecourt, in which was the pit containing pottery. All was then covered by the small oval cairn, and later by the straight sided cairn which covered the eastern chamber as well. The closing stone can be seen set back inside the two tall portal stones, leaving a small gap between the top and the capstone. An easier way in would be between the two wall stones on the south.* (Courtesy, Department of Prehistoric Archaeology, University of Liverpool)

higher up the slope. Inside this the excavators found prehistoric pottery fragments of similar, but later, type than that in the pit; and two broken pieces of finely ground and polished stone, about 2 inches long, with holes bored in them: the upper half of pendants. There was no pit by the entrance to this cromlech, but a pot had been crushed into the ground at the edge of the forecourt bounded by a stone wall. A wedge-shaped cairn, now vanished, had been built to cover both this cromlech and the earlier oval cairn. The chambers have been open for many years, and much has disappeared from inside them.

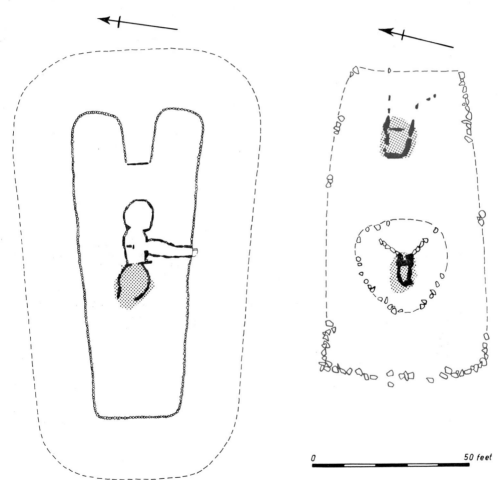

Fig. 5 *Cromlechau. Right: plan of Dyffryn. (Black) the earliest, western, chamber, and cairn. (Red) the eastern chamber and boundary of cairn covering both chambers. Left: plan of Capel Garmon. The dotted lines trace the probable edge of the covering cairns. Shaded areas: capstones. (Plan of Dyffryn by kind permission of Dept. of Prehistoric Archaeology, University of Liverpool)*

The finds from other cromlechau suggest what once lay in them.

BRYN YR HEN BOBL AND PANT Y SAER

The greatest number of cromlechau in North Wales are in Anglesey, many of them clustered along the Menai Straits, others where the limestone lies at the surface on the north-east coast. Almost all of them are on land which in the third millennium was easiest to cultivate, with light soil, free of heavy forest.

Bryn yr Hen Bobl was excavated before the war. Inside the chamber were found the jumbled bones of more than thirty people, including one small baby, a quantity of mussel and limpet shells, and the bones of ox, sheep and pig. Running off from the cairn to the south is a terrace built of stones, 330 feet long. Its foundations were marked out with pottery fragments and, like the cairn, it was carefully surrounded with a stone wall. The ground under it was covered with specially

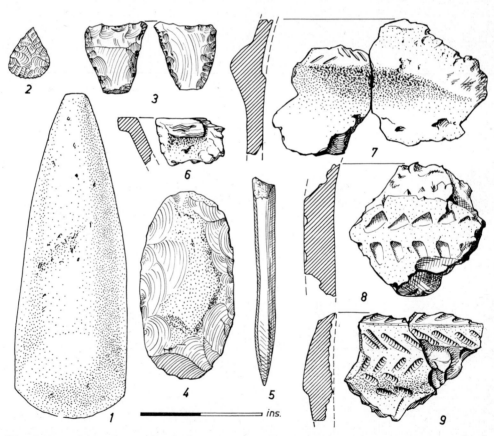

Fig. 6 *Objects from Bryn yr Hen Bobl. 1 and 4 Graig Lwyd axes, 2 and 3 flint arrowheads; 2 Neolithic A, 3 Neolithic B, 5 bone pin, 6 and 7 Neolithic A pot fragments, 8 and 9 Neolithic B pot fragments, 9 decorated with cord impressions ('maggots'). (After R.C.A.M. Anglesey)*

laid clay, in which charcoal was mixed, and this floor was marked with the treading of human feet.

The cromlechau of Pant y Saer and Llugwy on the east coast, like Bryn yr Hen Bobl had pottery in them, and bones of ox, sheep, pig and deer. They both held many skeletons. Pant y Saer had at least fifty-four, lying in great disorder, and with a number of skulls missing. Llugwy had thirty, and a dog among the animals. Both had quantities of shellfish on the floor.

THE NEW PEOPLE

Cromlechau, then, were burial chambers. They were used by people who made pottery and who kept cattle, sheep, pigs and dogs, and who hunted deer, all of which played some part in an elaborate funeral ritual. To build a megalithic tomb was no mean labour; it required numbers of people organized together for the work, and to provide food and shelter for the workers. The siting of the tombs near the coast and the large rivers (frontispiece) makes it clear that megalith builders travelled by sea. Their religion, in fact, originated in the Mediterranean and spread westwards, together with the knowledge of farming and other neolithic arts: pot-making, weaving and a special technique of using stone for tools (*neolithic* = new stone). This new culture was brought to North Wales by colonizers from Iberia and western France, whose progress northward can be traced on the map by their megalithic tombs, built along the coasts. Some seem to have come direct from Brittany or beyond, others from Ireland. There is no sign that farming was known at all in North Wales before they arrived; nor were cattle, sheep, goats, barley or wheat native to the land. The migrations continued for perhaps 1,500 years, and communications between the megalithic colonies were evidently close. The colonists brought with them, too, the cult of a Mother Goddess and of the spirits of the dead. Fires, dancing, and animal sacrifice as a prelude to feasting were part of the ceremonies of worship and burial. The forecourt or entrance of the tomb was often particularly holy, and was carefully blocked with laid stone after use. It is likely that a cairn or earth *barrow*, or mound, was always erected to cover the whole. The tomb might be built of megaliths or smaller stones laid without mortar (drystone walling), or both together. Sling, near Bangor, Llugwy cromlech and Glyn on Anglesey all use natural clefts, and caves were used as chambers in the Clwyd valley. Once sanctified, a burial chamber was used for a long period, the part of the covering cairn or earthen barrow masking an entrance being removed and replaced at each new burial; informal entrance was often made from the side. At Dyffryn there is a gap in the north wall which seems made on purpose for climbing into the chamber without disturbing the formal entrance (in the western chamber).

OTHER LONG CAIRNS

The Dyffryn tomb is linked by many of its details with similar monuments in Ireland; it is not alone in this. Other cromlechau near it and on Llŷn seem once to have had long cairns; whether they started with smaller roundish ones like Dyffryn and grew through later additions cannot be decided without excavation. Tan y Muriau, near Rhiw, also has several chambers, one a portal dolmen. The southern of the two Carneddau Hengwm is the same.

Tyddyn Bleiddyn at Cefn in Denbighshire is another long cairn with two chambers. It is the only built tomb in the east of our region, though caves, at Gop, Perthi Chwarau, Dyserth and Cefn were used as ready-made chambers. It held a number of skeletons, all of which had a peculiar shape of nose, suggesting that the chamber was a vault for men, women and children of the same perhaps royal, or priestly, family. A second, ruined chamber at Tyddyn Bleiddyn, entered by a narrow passage through the cairn, was full of human and animal bones: far too many to have been fitted in as corpses and joints of meat at one time. Roebuck, goats, dogs and pigs formed the sacrifice. Here then were forest dwellers, rather than cattle farmers or cultivators.

CAPEL GARMON CHAMBERED TOMB

One kind of long barrow was certainly not an extension of an earlier tomb, but was built to a neat plan (fig. 5 (*left*)). The best example of this type is at Capel Garmon. Here, beautifully restored, is a classic specimen of the 'gallery grave', a type built by farmer-colonists in the region of the Severn valley from about 2500 B.C. onwards. A little cluster in the Clwyd valley acts as a connecting link between them and a closely similar group round the Clyde and in northern Ireland. Capel Garmon lies on highish land and was built when the design of this type of tomb had been modified. The forecourt was no longer used to lead to the entrance, but was built as a dummy, and the entrance to the three-chambered gallery was made along a passage from the long side of the wedge-shaped cairn. A wall, straight sided, defined the cairn and forecourt, and over this, soon after the chambers and passage were built, a larger oblong mound was raised to conceal everything from view.

Trefignath on Holyhead, and probably the ruined Din Dryfol close under the shelter of its strange humpy hill, and Hen Drefor, both on Anglesey, were also gallery graves. In detail, however, they are more like Irish than Severn gallery graves, and are possibly several centuries earlier than Capel Garmon.

PASSAGE GRAVES

Another type of tomb, always in a round cairn or mound, has a long narrow passage leading from outside to the chamber. The type is among the earliest to be built in Iberia and Brittany. Groups of these passage-grave builders sailed into the Atlantic during the centuries between 3000 B.C. and 2500 B.C. and settled in the west of Ireland. The two best-preserved and most famous passage graves in North Wales are closely related to a group of very large and elaborate tombs built shortly after 2200 B.C. in the Boyne valley in eastern Ireland. The Calderstones at Liverpool, and Bryn Celli Ddu and Barclodiad y Gawres, both on Anglesey, are outliers of the Boyne group. They lie on the overland route by which trade in Irish gold and copper was carried to important markets in eastern and southern England and Europe. The expanding civilization of the Mediterranean cities demanded gold, copper and amber in such quantities that trading expeditions with trading posts and colonies in Ireland, Scotland and the Baltic were worth while.

BARCLODIAD Y GAWRES, A SEAFARERS' SHRINE

Barclodiad y Gawres, perched on a promontory dominating a good harbour, was perhaps the place of worship of a port of call, for it has little in common with other sites in the locality. The chamber is approached by a passage 20 feet long through the side of a round cairn, and is cross-shaped in plan. Five of the great stones walling the chamber are decorated with lines chipped with pebbles, in patterns of spirals, lozenges and zigzags (fig. 7.7). The chamber floors were scattered with cremated bones and charcoal, but not in a quantity suggesting a great number of burials. Ash lying on a large hearth in the centre of the chamber has a curious story to tell. It can only be explained as a 'witch's brew' concocted for elaborate religious solemnities. This is what was found: part of a pig's vertebra lay under the hearth; on it a wood fire had been lit, and when it had died down a stew was poured on the glowing embers. In this stew wrasse, whiting (both deep-sea fish), eel, frog, toad, snake, mouse, shrew and hare had been boiled together, with what herbs we do not know. The fire was then quenched by covering it with pebbles and earth, with limpets and oysters pressed into it.

Careful excavation showed that the side chambers had been screened by movable stone doors, and the main chamber protected by a guardian pillar standing in a niche. At its foot lay an oyster shell. The round mound covered a ring of peat encircling the chamber, and a kerb of stones surrounding this ring. The peat ring is unique, the other features are all close either to Irish or to Iberian practice. The patterns copy those on Iberial idols, and some are perhaps remote abstractions of

Fig. 7 *The ancestry of 'passage grave art'*. 1 *Syrian idol from the Eye Temple at Tell Brak*, c. 3000 B.C., 2 *and* 3 *slate plaques from Portugal. Early third millenium*, B.C., 4 *Stone plaque from Antrim, Ireland*, 5 *stone plaque from Neolithic house site, Ronaldsway, Isle of Man. Length 2 in.*, 6 *stone plaque from Graig Lwyd axe factory (length 6 in.)*, 7 *wall stone in Barclodiad y Gawres chamber, height* 5½ *ft.*, 8 *one side of pattern stone at Bryn Celli Ddu. Height 5 ft. See also patterns on lunula, fig. 34, beakers fig. 11, pigmy pots fig. 20 and Caergwrle bowl fig. 37. (1–5 redrawn from O. G. S. Crawford, 'The Eye Goddess')*

human figures. The links in the chain of examples, connecting them with east Mediterranean fertility or protective charms, and their change into abstract patterns, are traced in fig. 7.

BRYN CELLI DDU, A NATIVE TEMPLE

At Bryn Celli Ddu the ritual of construction was even more elaborate than at Barclodiad y Gawres. The chamber is D-shaped and entered by a 20-foot-long passage. This passage crosses a wide ditch which encircles the chamber and a large area outside it. This area is surrounded, too, by four rings of standing stones. The tomb held many burials. Both skeletons and cremated bones lay in the chamber and passage, some on a stone bench along the passage and round the chamber wall. A guardian pillar stone stands in the chamber, but there is no hearth. Fires had been lit outside and at frequent levels during the ceremonial blocking of the entrance. One small spiral was carved on one of the wall stones, some of which were dressed in the same way as the great stones at Stonehenge. Such dressing is rare in megalithic tombs. The solitary spiral suggests that perhaps other such decorations once adorned the walls, either in paint or on cloth or leather hangings which have perished. The important art which

has survived, however, is on the 'pattern stone' which lay, thrown down flat before the cairn was raised, behind the chamber (fig. 7.8).

The pattern stone is decorated with continuous zigzags of pitted lines, running over the top and down both sides. It lay beside the covering slab of a pit. The pit was carefully filled with special clay, and at the bottom lay a hazel branch and a burnt human right ear bone. The laid-clay floor of the circle bears the mark of fires and the trampling of many feet; the cremated bones of a child under one stone of the circle, and parts of cremated bodies under other stones and in pits at the entrance remain from a ritual now vanished and unknown. A large cairn was at last thrown over the whole monument, which in those times stood, exceptionally, in a clearing in natual heavy woodland. Figure 8 shows how what can now be seen at the site fits into the monument as it originally stood.

A SECOND NEOLITHIC CULTURE

Though it is clear that the passage and chamber in their round mound are typical enough of passage graves in Spain, Brittany or Ireland there are features at Bryn Celli Ddu belonging to another tradition. By 2000 B.C., when the Boyne tombs were being raised, the farming colonists from the Atlantic and

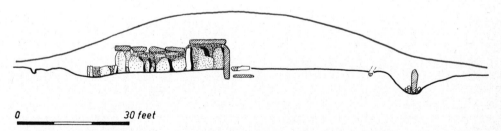

0   30 feet

Fig. 8 *Bryn Celli Ddu. A section across the chamber and circle, showing the pattern stone and slab covering the pit to the west outside the chamber. The passage crosses the ditch which defines the circle and holds two of the stone rings. The stump of a stone of the third ring can be seen within the ditched area. The fourth ring was well outside the area of the mound, shown in colour as it originally lay over the whole monument. A missing capstone at the portal of the inner passage is also shown in colour.*

western shores of Europe with their foreign traditions had mingled all round the Irish Sea with the original mesolithic hunting peoples who led a wandering life among the forests and along the shores. The customs and crafts of the 'western' new-comers, re-plenished by new arrivals and periodic visitors from nearer the Mediterranean, had naturally affected and been affected by the habits of the local population, whose cultural roots lay more among the northern European meso-lithic communities from whom they were descended. Early 'western' neolithic colonists can be recognized by the thin, fine paste of their pots, the earliest made in Britain, which are called for convenience neolithic A. But there soon appeared a rougher, thicker, highly decorated pottery, of which the early examples have been found oftener on sandy sites by rivers or where there might be trackways through woodlands than on lands then farmed. The makers of these neolithic B pots made mesolithic types of tool; for instance, flat-edged instead of pointed arrowheads (fig. 6.3), and they used string to make decorative mark-ings on their pottery as was done all over north Europe (a trick unknown among western neolithic peoples). They made much use of deer-bone and antler for tools and they bored stone for mace-heads and hammers as meso-lithic people had done. They improved their hunting life by exchange and trade with the less mobile farmers, and, as they grew in prosperity, their religious life developed. They made circular, oval or D-shaped sanctuaries, either a ring of pits surrounded by a bank and ditch, or rings of timber or stone uprights. They often cremated their dead and, like western neolithic people, too, sometimes per-formed human sacrifice.

No sanctuary of the neolithic B people is known in North Wales, but there are signs of their influence. Bryn Celli Ddu with its ditch, stone rings, cremations in pits and its

single flat-edged arrowhead, is indeed like a neolithic B sanctuary itself, with an added passage and chamber: even then the chamber is D-shaped. Bryn yr Hen Bobl is another example of the fusion of the two populations, for here fine western pottery (either plain, or decorated with delicate grooved lines) was found alongside the fragments of coarse stabbed or cord-decorated bowls made by neolithic B potters (fig. 6). Stone balls buried under the cairn are also characteristic of B people. Llugwy had both types of pottery. In all other excavated cromlechau the pottery was western alone.

AERIAL PHOTOGRAPHY

A photograph recently taken from the air shows two circular ditches near Llandegai, which may be a religious centre such as we have been describing. Aerial photography shows buried trenches and pits as darker markings in the grass or crop when nothing can be seen on ground-level at all. Many of the neolithic B sanctuaries in England and Scotland have been discovered in this way, as have other antiquities, such as Roman roads.

THE STONE-AXE INDUSTRY

The most important activity of these non-farming neolithic people in our area was the manufacture and distribution of heavy stone 'axes'. Immigrant farmers landing among the woodland needed to make clearings, break ground and till the soil, cut branches for cattle fodder, and shape wood to build houses, furniture and boats. A hunter or fisherman could obtain farm produce by providing the busy farmer with axes and hoes. So essential were these tools that specialist craftsmen were able to rely on their customers for the neces-sities of life and devote their time to making them. In the south of England they mined flint; in North Wales the volcanic outcrops round Penmaenmawr and on Llŷn provided excellent fine, tough rock which could be worked much as flint is worked. What we call stone 'axe-heads' were probably also used as hoes for tilling the soil at this period. Several polished axes, some broken, were buried at Bryn yr Hen Bobl, and many have been found on Anglesey, one near Bryn Celli Ddu. An entrance to the Gop Cave was guarded by an unused axe standing buried upright in the entrance. Inside were many neolithic burials, traces of fires, a neolithic B pot and jet belt fasteners, which have been found else-where on neolithic B sites. Another axe was similarly buried in a cave used for burials at Perthi Chwarau, Llandegla. The axe evidently was thought to guard a holy place with magic power. Other examples of this superstition are known among the megalith builders in the Mediterranean, Iberia and Brittany, who made miniature axe charms and carved axe shapes on the walls of their monuments.

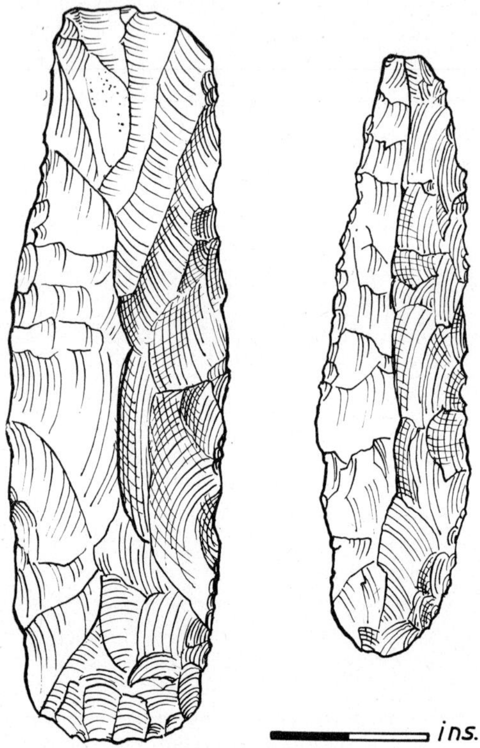

At Graig Lwyd, Penmaenmawr, and farther across the moorland round the heights of Dinas and Garreg Fawr the slopes are still strewn with the waste of the workshops. An archaeologist walking by Graig Lwyd some forty years ago noticed that the scree was full of rough or broken axe shapes. He then studied some 3 tons of the scree, which he found was full of broken and unfinished axes, adzes, chisels, and battered hammer stones, and of flakes and chips, some of which were fashioned into scrapers and boring tools. The difficulty in making the big axes was evidently to get the axe thin enough, and many of the rejects came to grief over this. Completed tools from the 'factory' site are very rare. When found away from the site they are nearly always ground and polished, so this finishing must have been done either at a separate centre, or by or for each customer, and there was no surplus stock. A few hearths have been found at the factory site, the stones surrounding them burnt by frequent heating. Near them were found quantities of hazel-nut shells, but the living-quarters of the stone workers are yet to be found. They must be hidden on the moor near some sheltered stream.

The stone in figure 7 with its zigzags was found at the workshop. Five similar stones with finely incised carving were found on the floor of a neolithic house on the Isle of Man. These plaques are probably all charms, like the idols in figure 7, for these are the same patterns that were used in passage-grave art. The broken, plain plaques found in the

Fig. 9 *Graig Lwyd axes and adze from the workshop. No polished tools have been found there. (Redrawn from 'Prehistory of Wales' by W. F. Grimes)*

24

Dyffryn cromlech may once have been painted with similar patterns.

THE STONE-AXE TRADE

The axe 'industry' grew apace, and implements were soon supplied not only to the locality but far afield. They are easily recognized by geological examination. One axe found in Somerset lay on wood dated by Carbon 14 to 2600 B.C. Another in Cambridge lay on peat of similar date or earlier. Most of the trade was carried on in the following centuries (fig. 10). In North Wales they have been found mainly on the north-coast foreshore, round the Great Orme, on Anglesey, in the Conwy, Clwyd, Dee and Wnion valleys. This suggests that they were mainly transported by water, which, in view of the weight, was obviously preferable to carrying overland. When they are found farther away, in Wessex, South Wales, far up the Severn, or in East Anglia, they seem again to have been mainly water-borne.

THE MYNYDD RHIW 'FACTORY'

Recently another axe 'factory' was excavated on Mynydd Rhiw, Bryncroes, on Llŷn. A number of hollows on the brow of the hill turned out to be shafts dug to a depth of about eleven feet, in search of the best rock. The stone workers, as at Graig Lwyd, picnicked and squatted round camp fires of oak and hazel wood to trim their tools, but again there is no sign of permanent living-quarters. It is interesting to find that while the axes exported from here to South Wales and the Marches are the same heavy type as those made at Penmaenmawr, those found together with other implements, such as knives made from waste flakes, at the factory, are all lighter axes. The excavator thinks these were what the workers made for themselves: scrapers and awls for skins; gravers, hollow scrapers and saws for bone and wood working; knives

for skinning and cutting the meat of the deer caught in the chase. The light axes and adzes would be suitable for trimming wood to make frames for fishing-boats, and perhaps for the beams and furniture for their now-vanished houses. The heavier axes from here have not yet been found as far away as those from Penmaenmawr, but since the workshop has only been discovered recently there may be many in museums and private hands which have not been identified.

Axes and chips of Mynydd Rhiw rock are known at three neolithic settlement sites where axes from Great Langdale in the Lake District and Penmaenmawr also appear. One of these is in South Wales, the other two are in Flintshire.

NEOLITHIC LIVING SITES: GWAENYSGOR

At Gwaenysgor, on the summit of Bryn Llwyn above Prestatyn, was a four-acre village, surrounded by a stone wall. The whole area was covered with a clay floor, and on top of this the inhabitants had dropped rubbish nearly a foot thick. Paving-stones covered the floors of wooden or skin huts, yards and pathways. There were many flint arrowheads of a rather pointed leaf shape (fig. 6.2) which is common in North Wales and the Isle of Man. These were found at Bryn yr Hen Bobl and Pant y Saer (where to judge from the quantity of arrowheads a salvo of arrows seems to have been part of the funeral ceremony), and at a neighbouring neolithic village at Dyserth. Among scrapers and other implements of flint and chert were scrapers and choppers made from fragments of polished North Welsh axes. A piece of shale ring is part of a small bracelet. There were many battered hammer stones, and anvils, sharpening stones and net weights. The pottery is all fragmentary, rough late neolithic ware. Ox, sheep and pig bones show that they kept domestic animals. A hollowed stone, or quern, and pestles were for grinding flour. Cockles were eaten, oysters more rarely. The excavator of Mynydd Rhiw has suggested that Gwaenysgor was the centre from which axes from Graig Lwyd and Mynydd Rhiw were sent off by sea after first being ground and polished. Ten broken pieces of polished axes among the exhibits from Gwaenysgor in the National Museum of Wales could then be the result of accidents in the workshop.

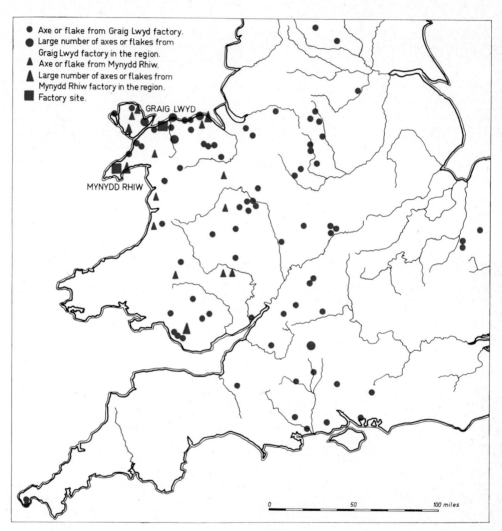

Fig. 10 *Map showing where Graig Lwyd and Mynydd Rhiw implements have been found in England and Wales. A very few have also been found in Ireland and Scotland. (By permission H.M.S.O. after information received from R.C.A.M. Wales)*

THE NEOLITHIC VILLAGE AT DYSERTH

There was a similar neolithic living-floor at Dyserth. On it lay flint flakes, cut antler, fragments of polished axes, broken pots, hammer and anvil stones, and the characteristic pointed arrowheads. There was much charcoal where fires had burned. Pieces of a bone necklace and a bone pendant spoke of more frivolous concerns. Dogs were kept, probably both for herding and hunting. We have an idea of the diet of the inhabitants. Horse, ox, sheep and pig, wild fruit, nuts and shellfish were eaten. Bones of a thornback ray among the fish refuse are an important indication of fishing from boats in the open sea. The axe finishers here depended not on the North Welsh factories for their supply of roughouts, but on rock from the Lake District; no Graig Lwyd or Mynydd Rhiw stone is found on the site. Two circular hut foundations were excavated. They had walls of stones and clay. Inside were several fireplaces and floors of hard clay.

DRIER WEATHER, AND THE MOVE UPHILL

The pottery made at Gwaenysgor and Dyserth shows that they were inhabited late in the neolithic period, after 2000 B.C. Earlier, people on the north coast seem to have avoided the high land. Axes, hammer stones, polishing stones, mace-heads, bones of domestic animals and the like, found lying below the tide-line on the shore probably indicate small farming villages on the islands which then dotted the estuary, and perhaps a port for shipping axes. Towards 2000 B.C. the climate began to grow much drier, and the sea-level rose considerably, covering the modern five-fathom line, which had been well above the tide a millennium earlier. This made a great difference to the coastline, as any contour map will show. With warmer, drier weather it was possible to retreat from the flooded fields to such heights as Bryn Llwyn and Dyserth.

Recently two more neolithic settlements have come to light. One is a neighbour to Gwaenysgor and Dyserth, at Llanasa. The other is at Bryn Gwyn on low-lying ground near the Menai Straits, on Anglesey. Here a stone bank and ditch protected a circular farmstead 180 feet in diameter. Results of the excavation revealed post-holes, probably meaning wooden huts; hollows, meaning storage pits for food; charcoal, meaning fires. Pottery was abundant, mostly of late neolithic decorated ware. The protecting wall was rebuilt much later by farmers of the Roman period who reoccupied the site.

4 The Beaker People

THE ARRIVAL OF NEW TRIBES

By 1800 B.C. or 1700 B.C. the descendants of western neolithic farmers and the descendants of north European mesolithic hunters had settled together to form a society combining, in its religious practices, the western megalithic tradition with the local British customs of circles and cremation. Burial in, and worship at, communal tombs was the established practice. Fishing and shipping went on round the coasts, much deer hunting in the woods, and agriculture on little patches of cleared woodland. As the uplands became habitable and the shore lands disappeared under the sea, more people took to the higher land, living there mainly off cattle, sheep and hunting. The axe trade provided the closest link with the outer world. The drier climate affected plant life. Where pine and hazel had grown unchallenged, oak, elm and lime increased in numbers and grew higher up the hill-sides, taking the place of bogs. Oak and lime are useful woods for utensils, and in the next 1,800 years pottery was hardly used except for placing with the dead. Wood perishes more easily than pottery, so we know very little about what people used at home until a little pottery came into use again during the Iron Age.

The drier climate must have been welcome in Wales, but it caused hardship in some other parts of the world, and large-scale migrations began. New tribes with new customs found their way to the British Isles, some from France, and some from the Low Countries. They had in common a special, often very handsome, type of drinking-cup which we call a beaker (fig. 11), and very likely the art of brewing some kind of beer.

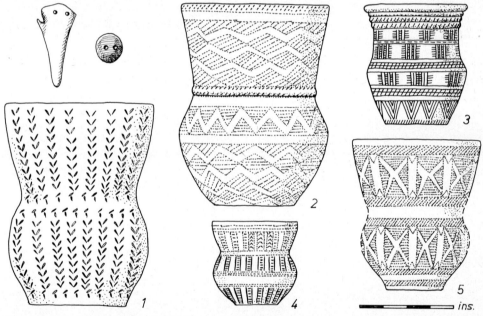

Fig. 11 *Beakers.* 1 *Merddyn Gwyn, Pentraeth, decorated with finger nail imprints. Above: the bronze knife or dagger, and jet button found with the burial. Usually the jet buttons found in beaker burials have the perforations in a V shape from the back, leaving the top unperforated, 2 Llanelltyd, in a cairn, 3 Mynydd y Bryn, Llansilin, with a cremation in a cist under a round cairn, 4 Bwlch y gwrhyd, Caerhun, with a cremation in a cist in a cairn high on the Drum, 5 Bedd Branwen, Llanbabo. The fragments were found inside Bronwen's urn, which was deposited in the British Museum after it was excavated in 1813 from a cist under a barrow. It is likely that the cist first contained an earlier beaker burial with an unburnt skeleton, and remains from this got confused with the cremation remains from the urn burial during the excavation. (Redrawn after W. E. Griffiths)*

They spread quickly across the British Isles and engaged in some trading. Many of them lived as semi-nomadic pastoralists, counting their riches in flocks and herds, like the Jewish tribes in the Old Testament. Some cereals were grown by them, however; a beaker from a cairn on Moel Hebog has fourteen imprints of wheat and barley grains, picked up by the soft clay from a hut floor.

Unlike their predecessors, they did not practise collective burial, but buried the most important members of their tribe, chieftain, priest or king, separately in a grave or cistfaen, sometimes under a round barrow or cairn. With the body they often put a beaker, and sometimes weapons as well.

A MERCHANT CHIEFTAIN
AT MERDDYN GWYN

Such a chieftain was buried on the hills above Pentraeth in Anglesey, together with a beaker (fig. 11.*1*). A flat copper dagger or knife lay behind him; it had probably hung from his waist. Behind the skull a beaker had been placed, we may imagine with a drink, long since evaporated, for his journey to the next world. All this lay in a coffin, or cist, built of large stone slabs and covered by a large block of limestone. The cist lay at the centre of a horseshoe of large stones, about sixty feet across the diameter. Over all this a cairn had been piled. The form of the beaker, and of the dagger, and a jet button which he wore are all typical of eastern English burials. Although our beaker man at Merddyn Gwyn seems to have come from the east, his people had absorbed something of the burial customs of the megalith builders in North Wales.

The Merddyn Gwyn chieftain lived, or died, in Anglesey presumably because he was concerned in some way with the beginnings of the copper trade between Ireland and Europe, either via the east coast, across the Pennines, or via Wessex (the growing trading centre for Great Britain) or both.

OTHER TYPES OF BEAKER BURIAL

Only one other beaker burial in our area contained metal. This was at Darowen, where two daggers lay with the body. Twelve beakers are known in North Wales from burials under mounds or cairns. One from high up on Bwlch y gwrhyd, south of the summit of Drum, is very small. The dead body was cremated as in Irish passage graves, and the curious ladder pattern is best paralleled in Ireland. Sometimes Beaker people fused so completely with the megalithic population that they used their chamber tombs. Pant y Saer, Capel Garmon and Ty Newydd on Anglesey were so used, and a small fragment of beaker was found inserted in each of the Dyffryn chambers. A few more beakers in moundless cists or pit graves, Scottish fashion, have been discovered in the lower-lying areas. A cemetery of three or more such burials was disturbed at Llithfaen during house building. A cist was uncovered recently at Brymbo when a drain was being laid, and the cist was transferred complete to the National Museum of Wales. The beaker is an early eastern type (fig. 13).

HEAD SHAPES AND BLOOD GROUPS

The shape of a head, its height and breadth compared to its length, is generally similar in a racial group. Another constant feature is the proportion of different blood groups in a community.

The new arrivals differed in physique from the neolithic farmers. They were taller in the main—at Llithfaen one of the men buried in the cemetery was nearly 6 feet tall—and the shape of their heads was different. Where the neolithic peoples were long-headed, with relatively narrow skulls, the Beaker skeletons have broader, rounder heads. They had stronger facial features with heavy brow ridges, stronger jaws and domed foreheads. Anthropologists have discovered some interesting facts about present-day physical types in Wales. It has been noticed that in the remoter parts of Pumlumon and the Black Mountains the population has an exceptional number of the B blood group. This proportion is nowadays generally only met with in eastern Europe. All the western peoples have a majority of groups A and O, and it is likely that these little pockets of B group people are of the oldest families imaginable, directly descended from Upper Palaeolithic ancestors. The people native to Pumlumon, where indeed there are very few traces of neolithic or later immigrants, are dark, with very long, high heads and broad cheekbones and prominent brow ridges and mouths. These features fit what is known of the Upper Palaeolithic inhabitants of the British Isles. The original inhabitants must have retreated before each wave of new-comers into these highland fastnesses.

Mediterranean colonizers were short, moderately long headed, smooth featured and slender in build, and they form one of the basic physical types in Wales. Their descendants mixed on the Atlantic coasts and in Wales itself with the earlier inhabitants to produce a type (recognizable also in parts of Scotland, Ireland, Exmoor and Castile in Spain) which is dominant on the Denbighshire moorlands: tall, dark and long headed, with narrow faces and features. Broad-headed tall people with marked eyebrow ridges, well-arched skulls and strong features are noticeable as native of the Bala cleft, between Bala and Dolgellau, and in some South Welsh valleys. Their measurements coincide with the skeletons of Beaker people whose burials are found in the same regions. B blood group is very rare among these modern 'neolithic' and 'beaker' type people. People of this type from the neighbourhood of Dolgellau can claim the handsome beaker from Llanelltyd (fig. 11.2) as the work of their ancestors!

INS

Figs. 12 and 13 *Beaker Burial at Brymbo. Now in the National Museum of Wales. The body lay tightly crouched, head to the north. A flint knife lies behind the skull. The cist is built of more than twenty slabs of thin sandstone. The capstone measures 5 ft. 6 in. by 3 ft. 3 in., and is up to 9 in. thick. The man was about 5 ft. 8 in. tall, probably between 35 and 40 years old. The beaker is decorated in continental style, with a cog-like tool. (Courtesy National Museum of Wales)*

5 The Bronze Age

BRONZE

Bronze is an alloy of copper with tin. The most suitable proportion, about 10 per cent of tin to 90 per cent copper, was discovered during the fifth millennium in the eastern Mediterranean regions where metal working was developed, but tin was not always easy to come by. Many of the earliest metal axes found in North Wales are of unalloyed copper. The Bronze Age lasted in North Wales from some short time before 1500 B.C. until some time after 500 B.C., when iron began to take the place of bronze and stone for heavy work.

CONTINUED USE OF STONE

During this long period stone was still much used and most skilfully worked, but bronze was preferred for weapons, light axes, delicate implements and ornaments. The collection of flint arrowheads found together on the high moorland near Llyn Bugeilyn shows what fine work was done in stone (fig. 14). The triangular barbed shape was introduced by Beaker people and is characteristic of the Early Bronze Age which followed, until spears supplanted bows. The flint of these arrowheads comes from Antrim in Ireland, and is one of the many signs of continued Welsh traffic with Ireland during these centuries. Local volcanic stone was used for heavy implements, combining axe and hammer, many of which have been found in North Wales (fig. 32); they are perforated in the old mesolithic manner. Like Graig Lwyd axes before them, these were sometimes included in burials, and still symbolized some magic power. Usually the buried ones were

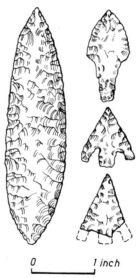

0   1 inch

Fig. 14 *Flint work of the Early Bronze Age. The arrowheads are typical of nearly forty found near Llyn Bugeilyn, Montgomeryshire. The knife, from Bryn Bugeilyn, Denbighshire, lay in a large Food Vessel with cremated bones, in a cist inserted into a round cairn. It is ripple flaked on the convex face seen in the drawing, the other face is flat and smooth, unworked except for resharpening. (Knife redrawn from R. E. M. Wheeler, 'Prehistoric and Roman Wales')*

rather small. The fine white chalcedony mace-head found near Corwen must have been a ceremonial mace of office (fig. 15).

NORTH WALES ON THE COPPER ROUTE

It is likely that Iberian prospectors were exploiting the rich copper ores of the Wicklow Hills in eastern Ireland for some centuries before the local inhabitants or settlers, many

31

Fig. 15. *Finely carved ceremonial mace-head of white chalcedony, found near Corwen. Three similar objects are known, two from Scotland and one from Staffordshire; they are all thought to be of Early Bronze Age. (Courtesy, National Museum, Edinburgh)*

of them no doubt employed to mine the ores, began to work the metal themselves. At last, probably through the efforts of the Beaker people, the secret was out. The rare ores of Cornwall were also discovered and worked, to provide the tin which could harden the Irish copper into bronze. The tiny trickle of metal objects that came through Wales in Beaker hands grew into a great stream in the years after 1500 B.C. The routes used by the early metal traders can often be followed as a string of cairns, stone circles and standing stones across the moorlands; often, too, as a modern trackway; many of the objects found by chance lie near these routes. The most easily traceable are those leading to Wessex from a number of landing-points on the North Welsh coast. (*See* frontispiece map).

THE DOMINATING POSITION OF WESSEX

Even in neolithic times the grandiose temples of Avebury and Stonehenge show that Wessex was an important centre, and we have seen how the stone axes from North Wales are found there in some numbers (fig. 10). With the development of the Irish copper supply a group of middlemen and promoters in Wessex saw their chance and started really big business, supplying Europe with British bronze goods, and no doubt other perishable commodities which we cannot now trace. The Wessex market attracted trade from far and wide, and by 1500 B.C. Wessex was plainly the commercial and religious centre of the British Isles. Wessex chieftains were buried with Irish gold work, Baltic amber and even Egyptian beads. A few similar graves have been found in Flintshire and Anglesey, as at other places along the lines of traffic.

THE EARLY BRONZE AGE:
BRONZES, CIRCLES AND BURIALS

After the Beaker invasions no sudden changes, and no drastic addition to the population,

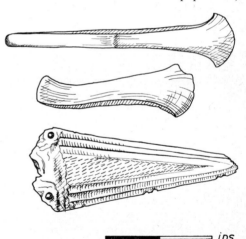

ins.

Fig. 16 *Flat axe heads, or axe (distorted by heat) and chisel, and grooved dagger found among burnt bones in Food Vessel (fig. 18). This stool inverted in the upper layer of a tumulus at Ty'n y Pwll, Llanddyfnan, like six other urns, some inverted, some upright. The chisel was probably mounted in an antler handle which also lay inside the urn. The dagger is a well-known Wessex type. (Redrawn after H. N. Savory)*

32

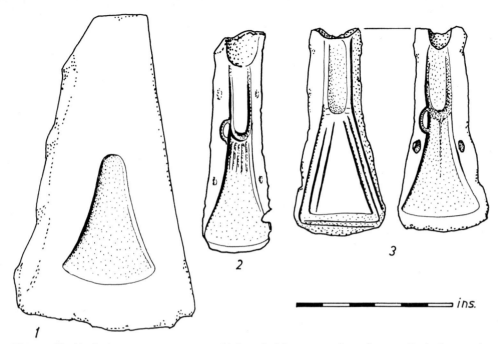

Fig. 17 *Moulds for bronze axes. 1 stone mould from Bwlch y maen; for a flat axe. Early Bronze Age, 2 Valve of bronze mould, found at Llwyn Mawr Uchaf, Parc; for looped palstave of late Middle Bronze Age type, 3 both faces of one valve of a complete bronze mould (found with another complete mould for a loopless palstave) at Deansfield, Bangor; for looped palstave of early type. Middle Bronze Age. (3 after R.C.A.M., Caern I, by permission H.M.S.O.)*

occurred until the last few centuries of the Bronze Age. For convenience the age is divided into three stages.

The Early Bronze Age lasted until about 1250 B.C., growing out of the intermediate Beaker period. Bronzesmiths made daggers (fig. 16), halberds and flat axe-heads. These were cast in open stone moulds. Axe-heads were thereupon hammered, to shape and harden the edge. It is known that smiths worked in our region, for a mould for making flat axes has been found at Bwlch y maen; it is now kept at the Old Fish Inn, Betws y Coed (fig. 17).

During this period gold was mined. It was apparently valued for religious as well as decorative reasons. The veins of gold in the Welsh hills may have been discovered (see map *frontispiece*) and certainly Irish gold work was carried across our region, both to Yorkshire, Denmark and North Germany, and to Wessex and on to central and western Europe, even as far as the royal tombs of Greece.*

---

* Recently doubt has been cast on the source of much of the gold worked in Ireland. Its chemical composition does not tally with that of the known Irish deposits. But even if all this gold was imported the work of Irish smiths still made their island the focus of widespread trading. (Information kindly given by Dr J. Raftery.)

Changes in burial practice introduced by the Beaker people and in time adopted in modified form throughout the population must reflect change in religious beliefs. Interpretation of the earliest known myths of Mediterranean peoples points to the rise during the Bronze Age of chieftains or kings who wielded religious power, and to the decline of the supremacy of the Mother Goddess of the earliest agriculturists in favour of a supreme God, or of a number of deities.

The new religion preferred open circles to dark cromlechau, its worshippers were often buried in hill-top cairns. Cremation, already usual in passage graves (page 20) and occasionally practised by Beaker people (page 29), perhaps under this influence, became universal. The neolithic ritual circle was adopted by Beaker people, who often added standing stones to it. Beaker-makers brought massive stone pillars from Presely in Pembrokeshire to the earth circle at Stonehenge and erected a double stone circle there, and all over the highlands of the British Isles they and their successors built smaller stone circles. Fragments of beakers have been found in twin circles near the Carneddau Hengwm. They both have a ditch and bank of earth, one 120 feet in diameter, and the other, with standing stones in the bank, 172 feet in diameter. Only two of the stones now remain standing, and the earth banks have worn away. By excavation the sockets of the other stones were found, but very little else, apart from an empty pit near the centre of the earthen circle.

We know little about the physical characteristics of the Bronze Age people, since their burials are all of small fragments of cremated bone. Many cremations were placed in an urn and deposited in a hole or small cist made in an earlier Beaker cairn or barrow. Very occasionally an urn was put in a cromlech, or in its cairn (Dyffryn, page 16). Some-

times a cist was built to hold the urn and surrounded by a ring or bank of stones. The urns were at first mostly of the type called 'Food Vessels' (fig. 18), which, in North Wales, are larger than beakers. The pottery shows the influence of beakers on late neolithic pot-making, with patterns often echoing passage-grave art. Flint knives, small axe-hammers or arrowheads sometimes accompany Food Vessels. Soon other types of urn were made: 'collared rim' are the earliest, then 'overhanging rim', 'encrusted' and 'cordoned' urns (fig. 19), types which lasted into the Middle Bronze Age. Fewer offerings were included with burials as time went on, so it is less easy to date them. Makers of Food Vessels set up the great Druids' Circle behind Penmaen-

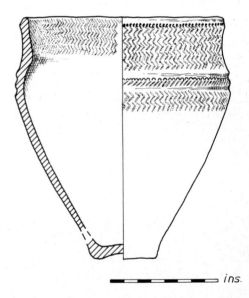

Fig. 18 *Large Food Vessel from Ty'n y Pwll, Llanddyfnan, found inverted over cremation ashes and the bronze implements in fig. 16. The tumulus was built of a layer of stones, then sand, over a core of gravel, and had a diameter of 90 ft. Nine burials were found in the upper layer, none at the centre. The Food Vessel is similar to pots found in Scotland.*

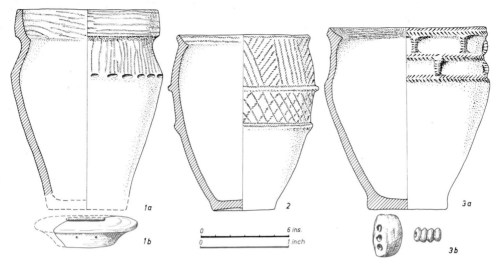

Fig. 19 *Bronze Age pottery.* 1a *collared-rim urn with characteristic dents round the shoulder from Rhiw, Aberdaron,* 1b *bone dagger pommel found with ashes inside* 1a, 2 *cordoned urn from Plas Cadnant, Llandysilio,* 3a *encrusted urn from Brynford, in which, among cremated bones and charcoal, lay the two pottery beads* 3b. *The urn is a Scottish type.* (1, 2 *redrawn after R.C.A.M., Caern III and Ang. by permission H.M.S.O.*)

mawr and many of the other stone circles on the moorlands.

THE MIDDLE BRONZE AGE: URNS, BRONZES AND MERCHANTS' HOARDS

The Middle Bronze Age lasted in our region until well after 1000 B.C. It is known almost entirely from finds of bronzes. Many Beaker and Early Bronze Age cairns or barrows, particularly in Flintshire and Anglesey, were enlarged to hold more cremation burials, with or without urns. Though the rite had changed since Beaker times into cremation, there was evidently no break in tradition, the earlier cairns still retaining their sanctity. Towards the end of the period burials were sometimes grouped in cemeteries without barrows. This new custom may denote the arrival of a new group of people. At Cae Mickney on Anglesey twenty-five urns and seven unurned cremations lay together in a circle. Other such cemeteries were at Menai Bridge and Plas Penrhyn. The urns here were mostly of the 'overhanging rim' and 'cordoned' types, common to the whole of Britain (fig. 19).

No domestic sites are known. Pottery disappeared completely as a domestic material, and was probably replaced by wooden vessels. The increase of lime and oak trees in the sub-Boreal climate made available good wood for carving into vessels and utensils, but nothing has survived. Deer-hunting and stock farming provided at least as much food as agriculture, and people probably lived in tents and light huts.

A novelty from France is a miniature pot for burials, called a pigmy cup (fig. 20); a number of these has been found near the coast in the north-west of Wales. They are often pierced with two or more little holes.

The skill of the bronzesmith increased. The flat axe was improved and given flanges,

35

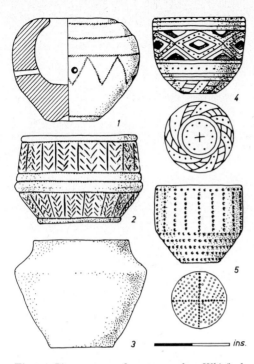

Fig. 20 *Pigmy cups.* 1 *from a mound at Whitford, Rhydwen, by itself,* 2 *from a ruined cairn, Llanelltyd by itself,* 3 *Porth Dafarch, standing inside an inverted urn, in the same beaker cairn as the pot holding the baby's remains (page 43). There is no report on the contents of this pot,* 4 *found in an urn near Bryn Seiont. The decoration on the bottom is also shown,* 5 *found together with a bronze pin among burnt bones inside an inverted urn, which was itself covered by an urn containing charcoal and earth. The decoration on the bottom is also shown.* (1, 2, *redrawn from W. Grimes 'Prehistory of Wales' by permission N.M.W.*)

which were made at first by hammering, later by casting in a double mould. Later still a stop ridge was added. This form of axe is called a palstave (fig. 21). Daggers were made longer, and developed into short pointed swords or rapiers; spearheads became common and bows and arrows seem to disappear. Spearheads were fixed on to their shaft with a socket, and made fast with binding attached to loops that were cast, first on the socket, later in the blade. Instead of loops there was sometimes a rivet hole through the socket. All these were cast in double moulds, either of stone, in Irish fashion, or bronze. Two bronze moulds for palstaves have been found at Bangor and one half of one on the hill-side above Bala Lake (fig. 17.2). Bronze moulds show the influence of central Europe on methods of metal working. This influence acted strongly in southern England, due to the closer contacts between Wessex and Europe.

Merchants tended to specialize in the wares they carried and would travel from a central smithy with a load of one class of goods: six rapiers in the Ashmolean Museum, Oxford, are all that remains of a cache of fifty found together at Beddgelert; another smaller hoard of rapiers was left, by a merchant who never reclaimed it, at Cwm Moch near Maentwrog (one spearhead was also found with them) (fig. 33.6); a hoard of palstaves has been found near Wrexham (fig. 21). All of these hoards are dated about 1100 B.C. About 200 years later at least nineteen palstaves were lost together on the hill-side near Mallwyd, and about fifty at Gloddaeth, near Colwyn Bay. Whether such losses were due to personal accident or to troublous times we cannot tell. The centralizing influence of Wessex was subsiding, and the dangers of travelling certainly increased, since weapons were becoming more frequent, but trading still extended over a wide area. Some of the maenhirs which stand all over the region are signposts set up during this period to direct travelling merchants.

THE LATE BRONZE AGE

The Late Bronze Age is reckoned from about 1000 B.C. in southern England with arrivals from Europe of people with new types of urn, and more important, cutting swords, socketed axes and a whole new series of bronze implements. They also introduced new methods in the manufacture and commerce of bronze. Consequently the south-east of England lost the close contact with Ireland which had been so important in the earlier Bronze Age. North Wales, on the other hand, was not much

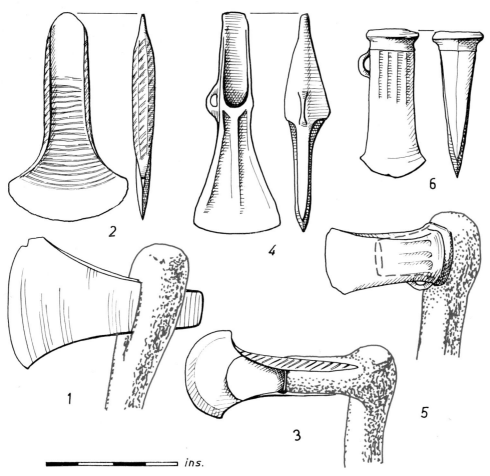

Fig. 21 *The Development of the bronze axe.* 1 *flat axe from Llanddyfnan, showing method of hafting,* 2 *flat axe with cast flanges, decorated in Irish fashion, one of eight found together at Menai Bridge,* 3 *unlooped palstave with decorated cast flanges and rudimentary stop ridge, Caernarvon,* 4 *looped palstave with strong midrib, one of four from the same mould found at Llanberis,* 5 *socketed axe found with a looped palstave at Llanberis,* 5 *socketed axe found with a looped palstave at Llanegryn,* 6 *socketed axe from Penllyn. The long, thin shape is later than the thicker shape of* 5. *All the axes when hafted would also be bound with cord or thongs.* (1, 4, 6 *after R.C.A.M. Inventories by permission H.M.S.O. No.* 2 *redrawn from Wheeler, 'Prehistoric and Roman Wales'.* 3, *redrawn from Grimes 'Prehistory of Wales' by permission N.M.W.*)

37

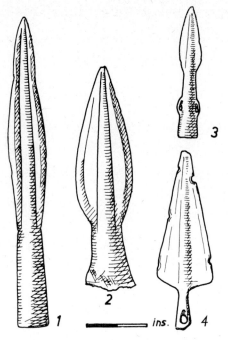

found in a peat bog at Arthog, where it had been deposited some time between 750 and 700 B.C. as an offering to the gods. Only one other equally early bucket (of a different type) is known in Britain; it was found with a hoard in Ireland. From such imports Welsh and Irish smiths learnt how to fashion splendid sheet-bronze parade shields (fig. 24).

FOUNDERS' HOARDS

In England, and spreading into Wales, large hoards of mixed bronzes make it apparent that in the Late Bronze Age it was usual for the smith to travel round among his customers, carrying his tools, collecting scrap metal and casting as he went. Summoned perhaps to a chieftain's hearth for some important job, he

Fig. 22 *Spearheads.* 1, 2 *from Eglwyseg Rocks,* 3 *from Montgomeryshire,* 4 *from a tumulus at Llanfachreth. It lay in a cist, probably with a cremation, and under a standing stone at the centre of a round mound. (*1, 2 redrawn from Ellis Davies 'Prehistoric and Roman Denbighshire', 3, 4 redrawn from W. Grimes 'Prehistory of Wales' by permission N.M.W.*)

affected by these changes for another two centuries, being in closer touch with Ireland and its clients across the North Sea. The latter became even more important to Ireland as the Wessex market waned. But in the eighth century changes began. New-comers appear in Flintshire and farther west, along the routes from eastern England. Others came from the south, up the coast, bringing the novelties from central Europe, including a method of working sheet bronze. The bucket illustrated in figure 23 is unique in Britain and must have been made in the Danube Valley. It was

Fig. 23 *The 'Nannau Bucket' found at Arthog in boggy ground, now kept at Nannau house. It is made of sheets of bronze rivetted together. The rings could hold a handle or bar. The bottom is strengthened with a plate which turns up round the side with projecting tabs for fixing. (Courtesy British Museum by kind permission of the Hon. Mrs Vaughan, Nannau)*

Fig. 24 *Parade shield, made of thin sheet bronze, with conical central boss and four small conical studs. Found upright in a peat bog near Gwern Einion, Llanbedr, near Harlech. Diameter 22 in. (Courtesy National Museum of Wales)*

would leave a cache of objects in a safe place, and he did not always return to find them. Stone, and even bronze, moulds would be heavy to carry on these journeys, often he used temporary clay or sand moulds. Thus the long-distance travelling pedlar was supplanted. Trade in bronze was confined to small regions, each with its own distinctive types of tool made by local smiths. Socketed axes from South Wales, Yorkshire or Ireland are quite different from each other, and restricted in their distribution. North Wales, with its relatively small population engaged mainly in sheep and cattle farming, did not support a strong, distinctive industry, and smiths copied Irish and English styles.

THE GUILSFIELD HOARD

The hoard of a travelling smith, containing 120 objects or more, from Guilsfield (fig. 25),

illustrates the two influences. It includes both broken or worn implements and weapons, and new untrimmed ones. One spearhead was carelessly cast, without the core for the socket, which is solid and useless for fitting with a shaft. A worn old-fashioned flat axe and several broken spearheads had been sold to the smith for scrap. He carried examples of both Irish and English styles of socketed axe, the continental innovation already universally adopted in England, and soon to replace palstaves even in Wales. But some customers must still have preferred the old ways for there are palstaves, one newly cast and untrimmed. The latest types of axe, spearhead and sword fittings date this large collection to the end of the eighth century B.C.

FIRST SIGNS OF NEW IMMIGRANTS

A large smith's hoard supposes the use of a pack animal, probably a pony; and we have examples of harness fittings (fig. 26.3–7), suited, it is true, more to a warrior chief than an itinerant smith, but at least proving that ponies were harnessed and in use at this time. A find of such objects comes from Parc y Meirch, Dinorben, and another from Anglesey. Here a personal collection of objects, mainly of English origin, was presumably buried for safety in the bank of Afon Cefni at Llangwyllog: tweezers, a razor (fig. 26.1,2), a wire bracelet, jet and amber beads and Irish harness rings and horse trappings accompanied a bronze disk of a type known from Yorkshire and northern Europe. Another hoard, mostly containing English types, was found at Ty Mawr, Holyhead, among the cultivation terraces and huts thought to have been occupied for the first time in the Late Iron Age, but on land thus apparently inhabited earlier. The cache consisted of two socketed spearheads (warriors often had several of different sizes), a socketed axe and knife, a chisel, a bracelet, rings and an

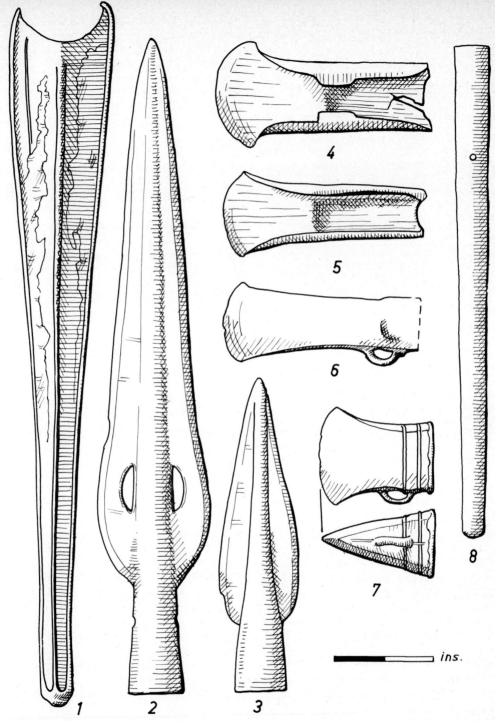

Fig. 25 *A few of the bronze objects from the Guilsfield smith's hoard. 1 sword chape, 2 and 3 spearheads, 4–7 axes, 8 ferrule, or casing for the end of a spearshaft. (Redrawn from R. E. M. Wheeler, 'Prehistoric and Roman Wales')*

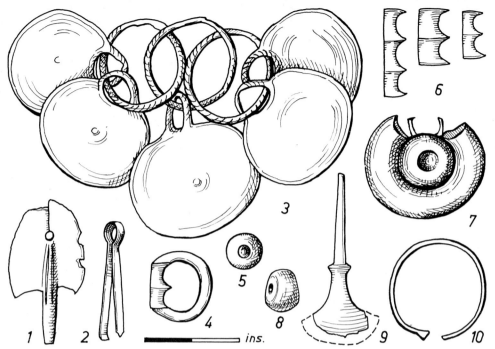

Fig. 26 *Late Bronze Age hoards.* 1, 2 *bronze razor and tweezers from Llangwyllog,* 3–7 *harness jangle, strap fittings, disk and amber bead from Parc y Meirch, Dinorben,* 8–10 *amber bead, bronze chisel and bracelet (in form like those of gold found on Anglesey) from Ty Mawr, Holyhead. (Parc y Meirch: Ellis Davies 'Prehistoric and Roman Denbighshire'; others: R.C.A.M. Aug. by permission H.M.S.O.)*

amber necklace. Intruders riding in from the east must have deposited these hoards.

After about 700 B.C. Irish gold work went almost entirely to northern Europe, and the trade route went across Scotland. At first, however, some of it still went across North Wales, as gold ear-rings from a cave on the Great Orme and ear-rings and bracelets from Anglesey show. A few isolated finds of implements of unusual form, such as a palstave with two loops, hint at continued connexions with Iberia; but from as early as 800 B.C. central Europe was in a state of turmoil from population pressure, with iron-using tribes from the east causing havoc among the old bronze-using societies. Our trading contracts

of peaceful times grew less, while refugees, settlers and marauding adventurers arrived in noticeable numbers, the later of them using iron. They brought European methods of defending their settlements, and the native population threw up defences against them. Hill-forts and fortified villages began to appear in the landscape. These, not burials and implements, are the most common remains of the next period, the Iron Age. But first let us look at some of the more important sites and objects of the Bronze Age.

BOILING MOUNDS

Large mounds, now grassed over, but consisting inside entirely of burnt stones and

41

charcoal or wood ash, occur fairly commonly in the part of our region most closely linked with Ireland: Anglesey, the areas along the west coast, and along the north coast as far as Conwy. These mounds lie close to streams, or on marshy ground, both in valleys and high on the moors. They are up to 4 feet high and between 30 and 50 feet across, and are crescent-shaped, with the open space between the horns facing the stream. The excavation of one in Anglesey and of similar mounds in Ireland has shown that they are prehistoric hunters' cooking-places. The early Irish laws make provision for 'hunting-camps' being free for all users; these are what is meant. The most thorough excavation of a mound has been in Ireland. Its description will serve for those in Wales. A central wedge-shaped trough, sloping to a depth of about 18 inches, lined partly with oak and birch planks, partly with stone, lay between the horns of the mound. The sides were packed with peat and moss. A large arc-shaped hearth was built at either end. Another stone-lined pit was dug and paved with flags, and nearby on drier ground, connected with the pit and trough by stepping-stones, were the post-holes of an oval wooden hut. The flagged pit was insulated against water seeping in, while the trough was arranged to fill from the marshy ground.

In 1953 an Irish archaeologist excavated several such mounds and established by pottery finds and Carbon 14 dating of the charcoal that they were used from neolithic times until the Middle Ages (from 2000 B.C. to A.D. 1000, or later). Not content with this, he rebuilt the hut with saplings, used the trough to boil a joint of meat and the pit to roast another, both entirely successfully. To boil a 10 lb leg of mutton, it was wrapped in straw and dropped into boiling water in the trough. For this some preparation was needed. The trough was cleaned and the gaps between the stones and planks filled with fresh moss. Clear water began to seep in. While it was filling the hearth was covered with a layer of stones taken from nearby rocks, then dry firewood piled high over them, then a second layer of stones. About an hour after the fire had been lit at one end of the hearth the first stones were red hot and could be used, to be replaced by new stones and fuel as the fire travelled round the arc. These stones were manoeuvred with a long-handled wooden shovel, and dropped gently at chosen places into the trough, now holding 100 gallons of water. In half an hour the water was boiling. The meat was lowered into the water, and new hot stones added every few minutes kept it boiling for 3 hours 40 minutes. In spite of the scum of ash mixed with fat, the meat came out clean from the straw and perfectly cooked, to be carved with flint or bronze knives and eaten with sticks.

FOOD VESSEL BURIALS: WOMEN AND CHILDREN

Whether women were admitted to such elaborate feasts we do not know. But women were held in some honour in Bronze Age times, for many were carefully buried. Shortly after 1500 B.C. the Merddyn Gwyn Beaker cairn was enlarged for urned cremation burials. A large Food Vessel was buried near the stone horseshoe wall, mouth downwards, as is usual in the Bronze Age. It held the ashes of a woman. Among them was the bone pommel of her knife, but the knife itself had perished. On Llŷn, at Rhiw, and at Marianbach, Cwm, in Flintshire, collared urns each held such a pommel among cremation ashes. This is a small detail, but it links the extremities of our region in a common custom. Handsome jet bead necklaces, widespread in Food-Vessel burials of women in Scotland and Yorkshire, probably accompany women in North Wales. One was included with bronze armlets and a jet button at Pen y Bonc. At Llong, Flint-shire, one lay in the small cairn piled over a skeleton. Here, too, was a memory of neolithic rites. The body lay over a clay-filled pit on a stone platform. The small cairn under the barrow is a feature noticed frequently in Bronze Age burials now that excavations are more carefully conducted.

At Porth Dafarch, near Pen y Bonc on the western shores of Holyhead, the crema-tion of a woman was again found in a large Food Vessel, which stood mouth downwards on a slab inserted into a Beaker cairn. Inside this urn, standing upright, was a small pot which had been lined with bracken leaves and which held the burnt bones of a tiny child and its pet dog. In Flintshire again at least one woman and child were buried in the same way, at Cefn Golau on Moel Famau, in a large Food Vessel with the pygmy pot inside. Other women, and babies, but not so close together, were buried in the same cairn. It is curious that the name of the mountain now commemorates a Celtic Iron Age god-dess who was worshipped in several forms at once, corresponding to love and fertility, motherhood and death, called 'The Mothers' (Y Mamau); it may be supposed that this mountain was a holy place, perhaps dedi-cated to the Mother Goddess, even in Bronze Age times.

BRONWEN'S URN

The Mabinogi of the Children of Llyr tells how a square grave was made for Bronwen, or Branwen, sister of Bran the Blessed, on the bank of the Alaw. 'Bedd petrual a wnaed i Fronwen ferch Lyr ar lan Alaw, ac yno y Claddwyd hi.' She died in Anglesey of a broken heart because of her ill-treatment in Ireland by the king her husband, Matholwch. Great was the excitement of antiquarians when a cist was opened in 1813 at Llanbabo by the side of the Alaw, and an urn was revealed. The cremated bones it contained are certainly those of a woman, and she may well have been a royal lady and even come home from Ireland to die. Unfortunately it was later found that the urn was placed in a cist built for an earlier, Beaker, burial (fig. 11.5).

FAIENCE BEADS

Many children also were given elaborate burial in the Early Bronze Age: whether natural death or sacrifice required it we do not know. A boy of nine at Garthbeibio lay with a mace-head or small axe-hammer of stone. At Llangwm two children were cre-mated and their ashes buried in Food Vessels. With them the great Flintshire archaeologist Canon Ellis Davies was lucky, and skilful, enough to retrieve two small beads of blue glazed pottery. He found two beads again in an encrusted urn, with a child and an ado-lescent cremation, at Brynford. These much-treasured beads are known mainly in Wessex burials.

The ribbed or 'segmented' beads (fig. 19, p. 35) are Egyptian, and a very important clue to dating the objects they are found with, for Egypt had now, of course, been writing records for centuries, and similar beads can be dated closely there. They prove contacts with the eastern Mediterranean about 1450 B.C. The other bead from Brynford, a spacing bead with three holes for separate strings, is likely to have come from Mesopotamia rather than Egypt. The trade routes across North Wales are only a section of a far-flung network.

THE DISTRIBUTION OF FOOD VESSELS

The majority of Food Vessels have been found near the sea in Anglesey; along the north coast, particularly by the Menai Straits; and in Denbighshire and Flintshire along or above the Dee and Clwyd valleys. These form part of an Irish Sea province which includes the

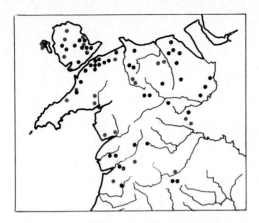

Fig. 27 *Map showing the find-places of Beakers and Food Vessels; red dots—Beakers; black dots—Food Vessels. (After H.N. Savory by kind permission)*

coasts of Cumberland, Galloway, Ulster and the Isle of Man. A number of boat-shaped graves also hint at the seafaring interests of their makers, who inherited and took over the trading goodwill of the Boyne tomb builders and perhaps of the stone-axe merchants before them. In the Clocaenog forest, an area full of tumuli and Bronze Age relics, a tumulus recently excavated covered two boat-shaped pits. Bronze tweezers, a flint knife, eleven arrowheads (very like the Bygeilyn Irish ones), lay with the food vessels. At Aberffraw the boat shape was laid out in stones. Above Llandecwyn a megalithic cist is rounded at one end and squared at the other (fig. 28).

THE PENMAENMAWR DRUIDS' CIRCLE

The most striking monument built by food-vessel makers in North Wales is the Druids' Circle behind Penmaenmawr. Tall stones stand in a circular bank about 8 feet wide. On the north the circumference is flattened to allow the passage of a trackway which must therefore be older than the circle. The

network of early trackways across the moorland between Conwy and Aber and the numerous cairns show that the axe-factory area continued to be frequented during the Bronze Age. It was not so bleak in sub-Boreal times (see fig. 1, p. 8) as it is now. Hazel, birch and oak grew near the circle in about 1500 B.C., and were burnt for fires. The peat covering the moorland has all formed since the building of the circle, and in these warmer, drier times it was grassy land, with trees much higher up the valleys.

Druids first appear in Roman literature as the priests of Iron Age Celtic tribes in Gaul (France) and Britain. It now seems probable that many Bronze Age immigrants to Britain, even perhaps some beaker-makers, and consequently their food-vessel-making descendants, belonged to a Celtic branch of the Indo-European, or Aryan, group of tribes which set out from south-west Asia during

Fig. 28 *Boat-shaped cist at centre of a cairn near the trackway above Llandecwyn. The cairn, now grassed over, is about 20 ft. diameter, and surrounded by a kerb of boulders. Probably built for a Food Vessel burial.*

the centuries after 2000 B.C. That is to say, they spoke a Celtic language. The customs of our Bronze Age population resemble in many ways those of the ancestors of the Iron Age Celts who later came from Europe as invaders. We may guess that their religious ideas also had something in common. Thus the Druids of the Celts would be similar in function to the priests and earlier priest-kings who officiated at Bronze Age ceremonies: the seers and priests of the Greek myths which picture the Bronze Age in Greece. But we cannot say positively that there were Druids in North Wales before the Iron Age, 400 B.C. at the earliest; and this circle was consecrated a thousand years before that. It was given its name in the eighteenth century A.D.

The Druids' circle has a burial cist at the centre, but it was not necessarily built as a tomb. Woodhenge near Stonehenge clearly had a child sacrifice at its centre, and at Penmaenmawr a child's ashes buried with a bronze knife in a food vessel appear to dedicate the circle to its religious purpose. The metal of the knife is not typical of Irish or of central European bronze, and may be made of Welsh metal. It is of the same kind as the Merddyn Gwyn and Darowen beaker

knives. Another of the same type lay with a food vessel in a much-used barrow at Ffridd y Garreg Wen in Flintshire. These knives can be dated to about the fifteenth century B.C., and the pottery style agrees with this date.

SMALLER CIRCLES, CAIRN KERBS AND HUT FOUNDATIONS

Many of the stone circles now to be seen high on the hills of Caernarvonshire, Merioneth and Denbighshire are 'cairn circles', the kerbs of cairns or barrows which have otherwise been destroyed, or which never stood very high. Others are the foundations of huts. These are one of the puzzles of North Welsh archaeology. They are so often found among Bronze Age cairns and along Bronze Age trackways that it would seem obvious that they are the remains of Bronze Age dwellings. Similar circles on Dartmoor have been proved so. Yet if there is ever anything found in them, and disappointingly often there is nothing at all, it is always debris and broken pottery of the time of the Roman occupation after A.D. 80. Many have not been excavated, however, and there is still hope of finding evidence that this form of building began in the Bronze Age.

Fig. 29 *Cairn circle, Bryn Cader Faner, near the trackway above Maentwrog. A ring of tall stones stands supported by smaller ones, outside this is a kerb of boulders. There is a low cairn inside, and a burial cist in the middle. (Photo: Miss J. Bowen)*

45

There are also a few circles smaller than the Druids' Circle, but, like it, neither cairn kerbs nor hut foundations. One such, with only a few stones remaining, is in Penbedw Park, Flintshire. Like most circles of its type, including the Druids' Circle, it has an outlier, or 'pointer stone': a single maenhir (standing stone) outside, standing at a little distance; and also a burial mound nearby. Another example, complete with outlier and burial cairn nearby, is the small circle on Moel Ty Uchaf above Llandrillo. This circle, in a district where numerous cairns show a populous Bronze Age settlement, and near an important track across the Berwyn hills, was perhaps a centre for social and religious gatherings.

The track at Llandrillo is the Fordd Gam Elen. It formed part of a route between the Tanat Valley and the coast, either at Harlech or up the Conwy. As it drops from the high moor to the Tanat Valley it runs not far from a curious little monument standing on a spur that juts into the valley about a mile above the Llanrhaiadr waterfall. A ruined burial cairn lies on a hump above the stream nearby, several cairns line the valley from the waterfall to the site and top the surrounding peaks. It is a double line of stones, between 1 and 2 feet high, 10 feet apart and 189 feet long. Such avenues, the most spectacular of which is at Avebury, are normal enough among Bronze Age cairns in other highland districts, and in our region there is one in Anglesey, one in Denbighshire and a short one on the Great Orme. This avenue leads into an arrangement of small standing stones, nowadays an exact semicircle.

6 Trackways, Ports and Trade Routes

Just as the Druids' Circle stands on an important junction of ancient trackways, so the Llandrillo circle dominates a route across the Berwyn from the Dee valley. Its descent at Llanrhaiadr is marked by standing stones. Thence the Tanat valley leads to the Severn, and so to the Clee-Clun ridgeway towards Wessex. Finds along this ridgeway suggest that flint was one of the commodities bartered in exchange for metal.

As we follow the map round the coast from south to north we can see how routes from landing-points ran up the main north-east-sloping valleys: up the Dyfi and down the Banwy, up the Wnion and down the Dee, up from the Traeth Bach into the mountain valleys. We will consider briefly each route and the remains found along it.

The Dyfi route starts with several Food Vessel burials and the hoard of palstaves at Cemmaes. Near Llyn Bugeilyn were found the Irish arrowheads (fig. 14), near Talerddig an Irish-type chisel of the later Bronze Age, and high up on Disgwylfa Fawr, where the hills of Ireland are visible on a fine day, a cairn was raised to hold a cremation in a food vessel of markedly Irish type. The urn stood in one of two hollowed tree trunks laid one above the other surrounded by a stone circle. Near Darowen was a hoard of weapons (now lost), and a flanged axe was found near Moel yr Henblys.

BROADWATER TO DOLGELLAU: VOTIVE OFFERINGS IN WATER

Another port of call was Broadwater. Standing stones mark the way on to the hills and across them to Dolgellau. Near the landing-place two Irish halberd-heads of the Early Bronze Age were blasted out of the quarry at Tonfannau. The track passes Llyn Gwernan, where a twisted gold necklet or torc was dedicated in about 1000 B.C. to the divinities of the lake. This is a reasonable guess: the number of gold ornaments, and other objects of value such as bronze cere-monial shields, found in lakes or marshes is too large to be coincidence. Classical writers of the first century B.C. speak of the Celts throwing offerings into pools, and the Bronze Age people of North Wales apparently did the same.

THE BALA CLEFT

Many palstaves and heavy stone axes or hammers have been found on the slopes lining the Barmouth estuary, and many cairns were built there—all signs of traffic and population. A cairn at Llanfachreth held a cist surmounted by a standing stone. Inside was a tanged bronze spearhead and a skeleton. Llanfachreth, too, is the find-place of another Irish halberd, made of almost pure copper. A cist at Llanelltyd held a fine pygmy cup and an urn. Nearby was the beaker burial already described in fig. 11. Across the water

Fig. 30 *Part of the ancient trackway between Bala Lake and the Tanat Valley, past Milltir Gerrig, facing a little E. of S.E. A the Bronze Age trackway, B the modern road. Behind the summit at the right of the picture are the Rhiwarth hut circles. Rhos y Beddau is two miles away to the east.*

at Arthog the famous Nannau bucket stood upright in a marsh. A heavy axe-hammer from Arthog has been shown to have been made in Pembrokeshire, of the Presely rock considered so holy that great blocks of it were moved all the way to Stonehenge. The axe-hammer must have been an object of prestige, or special power, because of its origin: local rock makes equally efficient hammers, and Presely is far away.

HARLECH TO BALA

Another clearly marked track leaves what was, before it silted up in recent centuries, an excellent little port at Llanbedr. Standing stones guide the traveller up to the side of Moel Goedog. The stone with a carved spiral, now in Llanbedr church, comes from somewhere nearby on the hill-side, perhaps from a ruined passage grave. A gold torc, found at Harlech, shows that someone had the means and opportunity to acquire Irish gold. A bronze shield was deposited upright in a bog at Gwern Einion (fig. 24, p. 39). The two small circles on Moel Goedog are cairn circles. The old track is easy to follow along the uplands above the estuary. A chieftain controlling this stretch of land could survey the whole southern coast of Llŷn and the approaches to the fastnesses of Snowdon from the rich valley below. It passes innumerable cairns and hut circles, comes down through Cwm Moch (where the merchant lost his small load of rapiers about 1100 B.C.), and is posted by standing stones across the valley, and on to the bleak moorland stretch to Afon Lliw, and so through Parc to Bala Lake. From the very source of the Dee, where a Late Bronze Age sickle (fig. 31) was recently found, this valley bristles with traces of Bronze Age occupation; axe-hammers of heavy stone, both on the hills and near the Lake, and the palstave mould from Parc encourage the search for as yet unlocated copper working

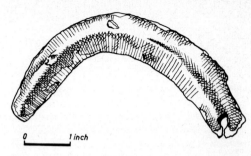

Fig. 31 *A bronze sickle found at the source of the Dee, Llanuwchllyn. One other is known in North Wales, and may be from the same mould. It was found at Dolbenmaen. Late Bronze Age. (After a drawing by Mr Ifor Owen)*

near Llanuwchllyn. Palstaves rather than spearheads or rapiers suggest peaceful agriculture and timber working rather than warfare. Nine bronze necklets and arm rings, like the Late Bronze Age gold and bronze ones from Anglesey in fig. 26, page 41 were found across the valley from Ffordd Gam Elen, at Llanrhaiadr.

Fig. 32 *Stone axe-hammer, found near the northern shore of Bala Lake, during drainage work. It is 7½ in. long, 4⅜ in. wide and 2 in. thick at the axe end. The perforation is hour-glass shaped, worked from both sides. (Photographed by kind permission of Mr Rowland Williams, Gwern Hefyn, Bala)*

SNOWDONIA

Other routes from the Harlech estuary led into Snowdonia and across to the Conwy valley. This was the martial region: Middle Bronze Age swords at Beddgelert in quantity, and later ones from Clynnog and Penrhyndeudraeth; spearheads, and another votive offering of a bronze parade shield on Moel Siabod. (Leather or wooden shields, such as have been found in Ireland, are much more efficient in use than bronze). Palstaves, separately and in hoards, and axe-hammers again suggest the working of local copper ores. At Danesfield, Bangor, two double moulds for palstaves (fig. 17, page 33) add to this evidence. Along all these routes lie the cairns of leading men and women, smiths, chieftains, merchants or priests.

THE TRANS-PENINSULAR ROUTE

The currents round Bardsey Island are notoriously treacherous, and traders evidently preferred to cut across the Llŷn by land. The distribution of maenhirs, cairns and boiling mounds and the find-spots of bronze implements make Brynkir the probable focus of the journey. The most spectacular find is a gold crescent, or lunula, from a bog near Llecheiddior Uchaf (fig. 34). These splendid ornaments were a product of the Irish Early Bronze Age. A bronze sickle identical with that found at Llanuwchllyn was found near the river just south of Brynkir.

ANGLESEY

Anglesey was highly populated. The island is dotted with cairns and standing stones which have not yet been plotted into any pattern of routes. Fishing villages, trading ports and farms must have been connected by a network of tracks. Irish connexions are apparent in finds of all periods. The gold trade from Ireland is illustrated by ear-rings or hair ornaments and bracelets made about

700 B.C. (fig. 26.10, page 41) which have been found at Gaerwen, Llanfflewyn and Beaumaris.

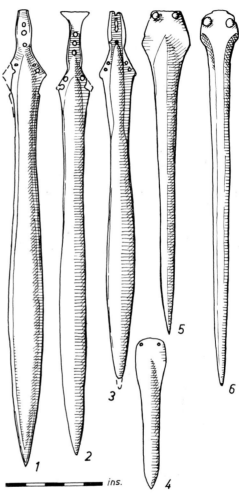

Fig. 33 *Bronze Age swords and daggers. 1 Penrhyndeudraeth, 2 Caerhun, 3 and 4 Dolwyddelan, 5 Ellor Garreg (found upright in a bog), 6 Maentwrog, (Cwm Moch hoard). The leaf shape makes a heavier, slashing sword. (1, 6 drawn from R. E. M. Wheeler, 'Prehistoric and Roman Wales'. 2, 3, 4 R.C.A.M., Caern I, by permission H.M.S.O. 5 Ellis Davies 'Prehistoric and Roman Denbighshire')*

49

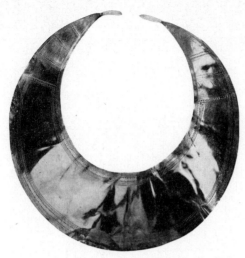

Fig. 34 *Gold crescent ornament from Llanllyfni. The only example in Wales of a 'lunula': certainly the work of Irish smiths, since about forty have been found in Ireland. The shape of the ornament and the layout of the decoration may be an imitation of a bead necklace (see fig. 35). But such dots and zigzags are often found on Iberian idols and pottery, and on some beakers and food vessels, and the influence could be in the other direction, the jet necklaces copying what may well be a head ornament of gold. (Width 9 in. Courtesy British Museum)*

An important route from the coast opposite Anglesey can be plotted behind Penmaenmawr. The Druids' Circle lay at the centre of communications. One track ran from Aber. It crossed to the Bwlch y Ddeufaen with its standing stones and went up the eastern bank of the Conwy to the Dee valley, crossing either at Corwen or Cynwyd (*see* frontispiece). The hinterland of Hiraethog with Clocaenog Forest, and both Eglwyseg Mountain to the north and the Berwyns to the south of the Dee, all have many Bronze Age cairns on their heights.

THE EASTERN ROUTE

Another route from Penmaenmawr ran eastwards to Derbyshire, Yorkshire and East Anglia, through Flintshire, passing a sizeable population on the Clwydian and Halkyn hills, perhaps taking in Penbedw circle. The precise trackways have here become obliterated by intensive occupation of the land between. The route is likely to have avoided the lowest-lying land, then thick with forest, and looped past Whitchurch and the potteries, as the modern road now runs, or else used the Mersey.

HORSEMEN FROM THE EAST

It is hoped, but not yet certain, that Late Bronze Age occupation of Dinorben hill-fort will soon be proved by excavation. In the fort itself nothing earlier than the Iron Age has yet been found, but at the foot of the crag a splendid hoard of harness fittings of about 600 B.C. was found among the roots of an old ash tree, together with crumbling bones (fig. 26, page 41). Strap slides, jangles, buttons and a curb chain all hint at the presence of military adventurers and horse-

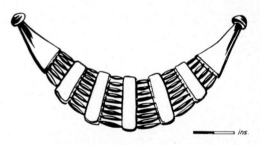

Fig. 35 *Drawing of necklace of jet beads found in a burial with 'urns' in 1828 at Pen y Bonc, Holyhead. Jet bead necklaces, often the 'spacer' beads decorated with dots and zigzags, are found with food vessel burials in Scotland, Yorkshire and Derbyshire. Such beads have recently been found at Llong in Flintshire in the small cairn covering a crouched skeleton. The body lay over a clay filled pit. Over the cairn was a layer of stiff clay, covering a standing stone at one side, and a stone kerb. This method of building a mound of several layers is characteristic of many Early Bronze Age burials.*

breeders, newly arrived from Yorkshire and beyond, who were perhaps attracted by the chance of looting rich trading expeditions. These horsemen reached Anglesey, where the Llangwyllog hoard already described (page 39) contained similar harness rings.

The paths used by these eastern horsemen were already well trodden by centuries of use. Moel Arthur on the Clwydian range was climbed by a merchant very early in the Bronze Age. In 1962 a schoolboy came upon three flat bronze axes of the earliest type, fresh cast, with no hammering. They were uncovered by a landslip after rain, having lain hidden under the soil all the way through the Iron Age occupation of the hill-top.

In the Middle Bronze Age, Flintshire was inhabited by successful chiefs, grown rich from the strategic situation of their territory. It dominated both the coastal communications with Scotland and Ireland at the north end of the Marches (the route between Midland forest and Welsh mountains, up the Severn and down the Lower Dee), and the only way across the forested Cheshire Plain eastwards to the North Sea. The great white Gop Cairn, which so far has yielded nothing to excavation, may have been built as a landmark, perhaps for beacon fires.

RICH FINDS IN FLINTSHIRE

One rich Flintshire chieftain was buried at Mold in a tumulus called Bryn yr Ellyllon (Mound of the Fairies), now built over. For long it was haunted by an apparition in shining gold which used to frighten passers-by at night. In 1883 workmen were levelling the mound when they came upon a skeleton, which crumbled to dust. Round the body was a great cape of embossed gold (fig. 36). Large fragments of it are now in the British Museum. Ashes and 'an urn' were also brought to light but lost, so one clue to dating is gone, but the decoration on the cape is likely to belong

Fig. 36 *A piece of the great gold cape, found at Mold. The decoration suggests a Mycenaean influence on the workmanship, and a date about 1200 B.C., though its similarity to Late Bronze Age embossed shields argues for a date several centuries later. The uncremated burial is unusual for any Bronze Age date. Height at narrowest part 7 in. (Courtesy British Museum)*

soon after the end of the Early Bronze Age, about 1200 B.C. The gold was shaped by hammering over a wooden patterned cone. It had then been riveted on to strips of copper and stitched to a cloth backing to make a cape. Several hundred amber beads lay over the body. In Flintshire, too, was found the finest, heaviest torc in North Wales; it had lain buried near Caerwys from about 800 B.C. until A.D. 1813. Another treasure was found

Fig. 37 *The Caergwrle bowl. Found in boggy ground during drainage work. It is just over 7 in. long, and 4½ in. wide. The wood is carved and inset with gold leaf, finely incised. The pattern evidently represents a boat, with a row of shields along the top, then oars (?) then water. At each end, below the 'oars' is a pair of 'eyes'. (Courtesy National Museum of Wales)*

in marshy ground near Caergwrle Castle. It is a small oval oak bowl, inlaid with strips and disks of incised gold to make a model boat, with shields, oars and waves, and pro- tective 'eyes' on the bow and stern (fig. 37). The disks are like Early Bronze Age 'sun disks' of gold, found in Scandinavia, using the pat- terns well known from passage-grave art.

7 *The Iron Age*

CELTIC IMMIGRANTS

By the seventh and sixth centuries B.C. there are signs that the peaceful life of lowland and hill farmers, enlivened by the visits of smith or trader, or by the passage of a chieftain with his retinue, was broken by bands of raiders and marauders who threatened the safety of the trade routes, and farmers' lives and storehouses as well. This danger was destined to become the normal background of life in the Iron Age. Defence of homestead and stock became essential, and soon the ramparts of forts began to rise on the hills.

In North Wales the Iron Age is almost a courtesy title. It describes the period after about 400 B.C. in which settlers kept arriving from the Continent, where the knowledge of iron-working was widespread, ending with the greatest invasion of all: the Roman. But although iron was known during the early years of this period, it was not necessarily preferred, and very few pre-Roman iron tools have been found in our region. Iron when properly forged is tougher and sharper than bronze. Its ores are much commoner, so that it is cheaper; but it needs more efficient fur- naces for smelting. For prestige weapons and ornaments bronze was still superior.

HALSTATT, LA TÈNE AND BELGIC IMMIGRANTS FROM EUROPE

In Europe the Iron Age has two main cultural stages. The first, named Halstatt, developed among Late Bronze Age Celtic tribes in western Germany, who adopted iron-working about 750 B.C. Their prosperity increased, their methods of cultivation improved and their numbers grew. They made heavy slash- ing swords (fig. 33, page 49) that gave them a military advantage, and their increasing population spread over the neighbouring lands, mainly westwards, since other tribes to the east were also pressing westwards. From the coasts of France some crossed to England, Wales and Ireland.

The succeeding La Tène culture arose from the impact of Mediterranean classical civilization on the more settled of the Halstatt Celts north of the Alps, who were now rich enough to purchase Italian wine and oil. The beautiful Greek and Etruscan vessels in which these coveted liquids came inspired the Celtic bronzesmiths to new artistic and technical achievements.

But war flourished alongside the arts of peace. Land grew scarce, and refugees, war- riors and craftsmen set out to try their luck in new parts, following the paths already traced by the earlier Halstatt expansion.

They moved into France, Italy and Spain, and many came to the south and east coasts of England, where there are signs of continuous arrivals. Each group brought a new or different aspect of the developing European iron-using culture. In south-west England the tin-mines of Cornwall and the fertile shores of the Bristol Channel were a lure to the invaders, and iron was discovered in the Forest of Dean. A few parties sailed on northwards, up the Irish Sea. The earlier immigrants, with their Halstatt traditions unaffected by La Tène culture, are in Great Britain classified as Iron Age A. Later landings by people with La Tène characteristics started off new cultures called Iron Age B. The divisions between Iron Age A and B are plain all around the south coast and in Yorkshire. It is one of the problems of North Welsh archaeology to fit our barren hill-forts and unusual stone hut foundations into the pattern of the Iron Age in the rest of Britain. One of the difficulties is that, continuing local Bronze Age customs, the Iron Age population made very little pottery.

The third wave of invasion did not touch North Wales directly. Iron Age C culture was brought by members of a European tribe called the Belgae, who settled in south-east England. After the Roman conquest a few of them fled westward. One of their princes, Caractarus, led the Silures of South Wales for eight years in their resistance to the Legions, and the fighting spread to North Wales, territory of the Ordovices, as well.

SOURCES OF WEALTH

'Poverty' is a word often met in descriptions of the Iron Age in Wales. We can find no traces of prosperous farms or villages. Yet some of the finest treasures of metalwork come from North Wales. Whether they employed their own smiths or bought the objects from elsewhere, the local chieftains apparently commanded some sources of wealth. If we could say that copper was mined in Caernarvonshire and Montgomery, copper and gold in Merioneth, it would explain much, but there is no certain evidence for copper-mining before the Roman period. Primitive tools have been found in copper-mine galleries in the Great Orme, which were worked by the Romans, and these may mean the mines began earlier. Lead was almost certainly mined in Flintshire before the Roman occupation. Some Welsh bronze objects contain a high proportion of zinc, and zinc occurs in some North Welsh copper ores. But this is only a hint. If worked at all, the mines cannot have been on a very large scale.

We can hardly imagine our area yielding vast agricultural riches, though the cornlands of Anglesey were important. Wool, sheep and cattle, trained dogs, ponies, deer hides and slaves may have provided the wealth to buy the fine metalwork or to maintain its makers. Leather craft may have been another source of wealth. Where traditional Irish stories make much of cattle and cattle raiding, the Welsh stories refer often to leather working: shields, saddles and shoes of finely worked leather make Manawydan and Pryderi rich. Wood carving, like the embossing of leather, may lie behind the designs used by the bronzesmith. It may be noticed also that these heroes and their companions are constantly on the move, a way of life born out in archaeology by the absence of dwellings, other than the cramped huts of hill-forts. There is no mention in ancient Welsh or Irish literature of pottery, but there is frequent reference to cauldrons and feasting. The tankard found at Trawsfynydd (fig. 38) is made of staves of yew wood, sheeted with bronze and mounted with a bronze handle of fine Celtic workmanship, with its typically

Fig. 38 *The Trawsfynydd Tankard. Made of staves of yew wood, plated with bronze. Nearly 5 in. high. (Courtesy, City of Liverpool Museum)*

asymmetrical design. Most tankards were probably of wood alone. This preference for leather or metal or wood explains why, even if immigrants arrived with the custom of pottery-making, they soon changed to local customs, and ceased to make it.

CASTELL ODO, AN EARLY IRON AGE VILLAGE

An example, perhaps more drastic than usual, of this abandonment of pottery-making can be seen at Castell Odo, on Mynydd Ystum, near Aberdaron. The first settlers on the site came from overseas. They made very rough storage jars of pottery, imitating the shouldered form of Halstatt bronze buckets in local clay, which they built up in coils, the method used ever since neolithic times. Further indication of their foreign origin is the fact that they built with wood. Rows of post-holes, seen by the excavators as pockets of finer, differently coloured earth in the old ground surface, remain from the timber used for huts and fencing. The natural building material of the region was, as now, stone. Wood had to be

fetched from 20 miles or more inland. These were Iron Age A people, some of whom, to judge by distinctive details in the pottery, sailed on and settled in the Shetlands. This group was the more fortunate, for the settlers on Llŷn were attacked and driven out. Some time after the foundation of the village there was threat of danger, and work began on a heavy stockade, bedded in a trench. But before the defence was finished the structures were burnt to the ground. The site was taken over by builders of stone huts, most likely 'Bronze Age' natives, who threw up a rampart of stones and earth round their new village. Little pottery was made after this. Perhaps some of the women of the first village were kept as slaves, or wives, because a small amount of pottery was found in the second village, but the craft soon died out entirely.

Similar Iron Age A immigrants settled on Parc y Meirch, Dinorben and Moel Hiraddug during the fourth century B.C., or earlier. At Dinorben the village was again destroyed, at Moel Hiraddug the settlers prospered.

THE BEGINNINGS OF LA TÈNE ART

La Tène metalwork appears in Wales and Ireland in the years after 300 B.C.: the first signs of the presence of Iron Age B chieftains. The earliest piece of metalwork decorated in La Tène style to be found in North Wales is the bronze bowl from a cist at Cerrig y

Fig. 39 *Portion of the underside of the flange of the bowl from Cerrig y Drudion. The stiff classical palmette is already asymmetrical, but has not achieved the freedom of later Celtic design. (Courtesy National Museum of Wales)*

Fig. 40 *Three-legged, or* triskele *ornament embossed on the plaque found with shield and sword fragments under the fallen rampart at Moel Hiraddug. This is a more symmetrical version of the* triskele *than the Tal y Llyn examples, but it is full of movement. (The original has been lost from the Powysland Museum, Welshpool)*

Drudion. The bowl was made for hanging and the design is all on the underside (fig. 39). The stylized leaf pattern, or 'palmette' on the flange shows an early (third century) stage in Celtic art, before craftsmen in Britain developed the full asymmetrical freedom of the *triskeles* on the Hiraddug plaque (fig. 40), the Tal y Llyn shield boss (fig. 41) or the tendrils on the handle of the Trawsfynydd tankard, which were all probably made in the first century B.C.

THE FIRST WALLED HILL-FORTS

Iron Age B invaders did not at first come in sufficient numbers to build forts, but marauding bands were troublesome enough to cause the earlier native population and older Iron Age settlers to throw up defences against them. The early stone-walled forts, Carn

Boduan, Carn Fadrun, Craig y Dinas on Llŷn, Dinorwig near the Straits, Caer Lleion on Conwy Mountain, Pen y Gaer on the Conwy, Dinorben and Moel Hiraddug on the Clwyd, were built in perturbed times around

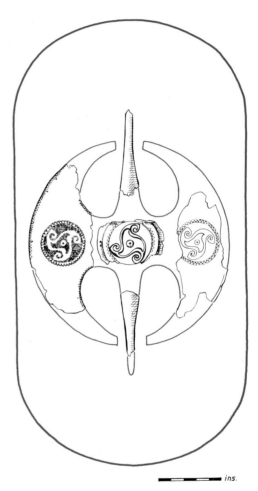

Fig. 41 *The Tal y Llyn shield (reconstruction after Dr H. M. Savory). The triskele ornament on the right is badly preserved. The shape and central attachment are similar to the shield from Moel Hiraddug, found with the decorated plaque fig. 40. (By kind permission Messrs Idris Ltd.)*

300 B.C. In some westerly forts and at Moel Hiraddug, solid circular stone huts indicate permanent occupation. Others perhaps were rather temporary refuges for villagers from the valley or for wandering shepherds in the summer season of tribal warfare and highland pasturage. The Clwydian forts are akin to the many forts on the Marches (the border-land between England and Wales). Movements overland from Wessex and the Severn mouth may account for more arrivals here than the western seaways which connect the west of our region with Cornwall, Brittany, and farther south in Europe.

MOEL HIRADDUG

Moel Hiraddug was an Iron Age A chieftain's stronghold. The relics of occupation in the hill-fort, above the earlier undefended village, are numerous, and Iron Age A pottery did not die out as it had farther west; iron, bone and antler were worked, corn was ground on saddle querns. The presence here of stone huts, typical on forts west of Conwy, perhaps mean that this chieftain came from there, not up the Marches. Later in its history there was trouble. Fragments of a bronze sword, a shield and some bronze plates which are possibly the decoration of a vehicle (fig. 40, page 55) have been found under a collapsed rampart near the bottom of the defence ditch cut into the rock. They are the work of a smith working in the Iron Age B tradition. The pattern of the plate in fig. 40 is a version of the three-legged magical triskele, descended from the Bronze Age sun disks of Scandinavia, and much used in Celtic art. The design was produced by hammering over a metal die cast from a wooden model. Wood carving itself must have had many master craftsmen whose work has all perished.

This find hints at an attack by Iron Age B warriors early in the first century B.C. The wall was rebuilt after the attack and the gate-way improved, and occupation continued until the Romans arrived.

A SUCCESSFUL IRON AGE B INVASION, AND A SECOND PHASE OF FORT BUILDING

The Veneti in Brittany are known to have taken possession of the Cornish tin supplies towards the end of the second century. The incident at Moel Hiraddug is among many signs of military activity in North Wales at this time. Both troubles and artistic developments were stimulated by contacts with the Continent. Earlier walled forts like Carn Boduan, Carn Fadrun and Caer Lleion were strengthened against an invader, and a number of new ones were built, both on Anglesey and on the hills of the mainland, among them Tre'r Ceiri (fig. 42). The invaders made an effective landing on the north-west, for they, too, built a series of forts. These were of a new kind with several wide earth ramparts and ditches. All of these newcomers' forts are close to the coast, two of them, Din-llaen and Dinas Dinlle, dominating good landing-places. These must mark the bridge-heads by which this Iron Age B invasion was launched, and from which the invaders managed to capture several of the defenders' walled forts and fortify them in their own way: Craig y Dinas at Llanllyfni and Dinor-wig are the most impressive of these. And it is probably at this moment that Pen y Gaer at Llanbedr y Cennin, with its spiked stone ground defence (*chevaux de frise*) was rebuilt with broad earthen ramparts covering the earlier walled defences. Widely spaced double ramparts with *chevaux de frise* protection are known in western Ireland and are common in Spain. Their builders perhaps all had a common origin. Caer Engan and Y Foel, both near Craig y Dinas, Llanllyfni, are also newly built double-ramparted forts, and some forts along the Merioneth coast probably belong to the same period: Pen Dinas,

Fig. 42 *Air photograph of Tre'r Ceiri, looking up to the cairn at the north-east end. The main entrance is at the south-west. Hut circles and field walls can be seen outside the great walls, as well as the town of huts inside. (Courtesy, Cambridge University Committee for Aerial Photography)*

Llanaber, near which two Iron Age B bronze horse bits were found, Moel Goedog, Byrllysg and Castell Mawr, Llangelynin. Against them perhaps the walled forts of Craig y Dinas Llanaber and Craig y Dinas at Llanddwywe were raised. Farther inland, fort builders were spreading from the Severn valley and the Marches up the Tanat, and up the Dee to Caer Euni, Caer Drewyn and the hill-tops at the head of the River Clwyd.

THE HILL-FORT AT DINORBEN

Much excavation has recently taken place on Parc y Meirch, Dinorben. Four stages of occupation have been disentangled, with their approach road and defences built one over the other. The first was an unfortified village like the first Castell Odo. Then the hill-top was protected by Iron Age A defenders, about 300 B.C., with a single bank and ditch. A gravelled road led through a gap in the ramparts which was defended with a heavy wooden gate. The heads of captives taken in fighting can be imagined adorning this gate from time to time. In the first century B.C. more elaborate defences were constructed over the destroyed ruins of the earlier rampart. The new occupiers dug wide ditches (such as are usual defending the hill-forts of the Severn valley) on all but the precipitous western side. Pen y Corddyn, Caer Euni, Moel Fenlli, Caer Drewyn are a few others which were given wide military ditches at this time. The territory was thus apparently divided among a number of petty chieftains, none much more powerful than the rest, and this lack of centralized power probably explains why the Romans found easy victory over the Deceangli during the years before A.D. 51.

The second fort at Dinorben again was destroyed, and a few huts were later built on the site above the fallen ramparts. The destroyers here must be the Roman army.

LATER HISTORY OF CASTELL ODO

Castell Odo did not become a fort. It was taken over by stone-hut builders well before 300 B.C. and enclosed with a bank of earth and rubble, such as might surround a farmstead, about 8 or 10 feet wide and 5 feet high (Stage 2). A century or so later, presumably when invaders were causing unrest again, the bank was given a facing of stone, and another outer bank thrown up and walled with stone. Between these banks was suitable shelter for cattle or sheep. A cobbled track led through the entrances of the two banks, through gates swung on posts standing in holes cut in the rock. This peaceful cattle farm continued for several generations (Stage 3), until suddenly the banks were pulled down and the large stones in them dragged away. Rubble was used to raise the roadway leading in through the gap. In time huts were built over the ruined banks (Stage 4). This is the same drama we have seen at Dinorben. In the years after A.D. 78 the Roman army was determined to leave no possible centres for native opposition. A detail of detective work confirms this explanation. A perfectly intact 'saddle' quern (hollowed stone used to grind flour) was used in the latest, fourth stage, to pave a hut floor. The only reason for discarding the quern would be that new rotary querns (dome-shaped mills worked by rotary action) were already in use. These were introduced by the Romans.

HUTS

Stone huts, both in hill-forts and in isolated settlements, are widespread west of the Conwy. East from the valley (with the exception of Moel Hiraddug) there are only clusters of circular banks. In these on Brynford Mountain, Derwen and Clocaenog moors, and a few other sites in Denbighshire, wooden or daub and wattle huts were built instead. Such huts filled the fort at Dinorben. They were difficult to excavate because they were built on levelled platforms dug into the sloping hill-side, and the outer half has often been washed away, but rings of holes and the central roof post-hole make it clear that the roof in these huts was held on an inner ring of wooden pillars. Gullies were cut into the rock to drain rainwater out of the living-quarters. Posts at the doorway held a door. Pen y Gaer, Llanaelhaearn, unlike most western walled forts, has no stone huts, only platforms with no sign of walls. At Caer Lleion a round hut built in one with the defence wall contained more than 400 sling stones collected from the beach. Sling stones have only been discovered at one other fort in Caernarvonshire, in a hut on Carn Boduan, otherwise they are found in the Clwyd forts. The builders of the multi-ramparted forts did not build stone huts, which belong to the walled-fort tradition.

'ENCLOSED HUT GROUPS'

Stone huts were either built of small coursed stones or of large upright boulders with smaller stones between. The latter method was used frequently for the 'enclosed' or walled farmsteads, the rooms and barns often built in one with the wall round a courtyard (fig. 43), inhabited during the Roman occu-pation. The shape of house, barn or of enclosing wall may be round or straight. Straight lines are commonest in the neigh-bourhood of the Roman fort at Segontium, and are presumed to show contact with Roman culture. The builders of these houses chose dry, sloping sites near the 600-foot contour, and the slope seems more important to them than a sheltered or sunny position. The houses usually lie among fields marked by straight terraces. The terraces sometimes survive when the huts have disappeared. The terraces formed as a result of ploughing along the slope of the hillside, after a strip had been cleared by rolling the stones to its lower edge. Over the years the top soil worked level to the top of this stone wall. Good examples of these terraces can be seen close to the Caernarfon road at Caerau, on the hill-side east of Llanaelhaearn, or up the Sgethin south of Dyffryn. One explanation of these distinctive farmsteads is that they housed people brought in from overseas by the Romans to repopulate the area after the Ordovices were wiped out in battle in A.D. 78.

'UNENCLOSED' HUTS

The more traditional farmers lived in stone-built huts or small houses without a surround-ing wall, often grouped in small steadings.

Fig. 43 *Muriau'r Gwyddelod (Irishmens' Walls) above Harlech. The walls stand to a height of 4 ft. A few of the rooms and sheds which were once built in the thickness of the wall can still be made out, giving on to the central large courtyard which may well also have contained buildings. A field wall runs away to the right. The entrance is to the left, near the electric poles. Probably built during the Roman occupation.*

They are simple circular foundations, sometimes with an entrance porch or a small side room attached. Remains of these are found now on the higher and poorer land, but the better land has always been in use since, and they may once have stood there, too, and been replaced by later farms and villages. Unenclosed huts often lie among low, ruined walls, presumably once the base of brushwood or timber fences. They enclose irregular patches, some for garden plots, others for penning animals. Where these dwellings were not highland *hafotai* (seasonal dwellings for summer pasturage) with no agriculture, cultivation was all done by hand. The absence of pottery in all the huts of this type shows how little Roman civilization affected these farmers. Some indeed are likely to be pre-Roman, but others were not. Whether he lived in flimsy huts, now vanished, or in simple round huts with stone foundations, the life of the small farmer and the shepherd remained much the same from the Late Bronze Age right through the Roman occupation and after. Their labour provided the food for the Celtic nobles, whose warring, feasting and worship demanded the maintenance or payment of skilled armourers, smiths and wood- and leather-workers, and for the priests who played so important a part in Iron Age Celtic society.

THE CELTS

Descriptions by classical writers of the Celts in Gaul apply equally well to the Britons. From these writers we have a vivid picture of the excitable warlike Celts, wearing trousers, or gay woven tunics and cloaks which they removed for battle, plastering their tawny hair with lime to make it stand out stiff like a mane. They were great drinkers, fond of music and story-telling, quick to pick a quarrel and equally quick to abandon it, hospitable and generous and politically unstable, tribe making

and breaking agreement with tribe, or with the Roman authority, as the whim took it. When Agricola became Governor of Britain in A.D. 78 the most important tribe in North Wales was the *Ordovices*. Dinorwig probably preserves their name, and if this is so the Ordovices were arriving in North Wales during the second century B.C. The *Deceangli* were in Flintshire. The Anglesey place-names of Din Silwy and Llanfair Ynghornwy look like memorials of the *Selgovae* and *Cornovii*; but where all these tribes came from, how long they had been here and whether they arrived as invaders or quiet colonists, we do not know. From Caesar we know that Anglesey was the main Druid centre, and the historian Tacitus describes Anglesey as a place full of sacred groves, inhabited by a warlike people, and a common refuge for all discontented Britons. Here is his account of the scene at the battle of the Menai Straits in A.D. 61, when the Roman army first penetrated into Snowdonia. 'On the opposite shore stood the Britons, in serried ranks, and prepared for action. Women were seen rushing through the ranks in wild disorder; their apparel funereal; their hair loose to the wind; in their hands flaming torches and their whole appearance resembling the frantic rage of the Furies. The Druids were ranged in order, with hands uplifted, invoking the gods, and pouring forth horrible curses.'

THE DRUIDS: PRIESTS, TEACHERS AND MAGICIANS OF THE CELTS

Accounts of the Druids give varied pictures of their character. Young men of the leading families were sent to Anglesey even from Gaul to be instructed in religion. This included learning the tribal laws, history, astronomy and philosophy. All of this learning was by heart, for there were no books. Although some Druids who came into touch with the Romans were literate in Latin, the sacred teaching had to be handed down in the traditional way. Bards, too, were trained in the recitation of tribal lore and history. This is how the bards in later centuries preserved old fragments even of Bronze Age traditions in such stories as the Mabinogion or the Book of Taliesin, and the Irish legends. Caesar's Gaulish friend, the Druid Divitiacus, was evidently a civilized intellectual, but there was another side to Druidism, which had its roots in more savage traditions. Belief that after death the soul passes from one body into another perhaps justified to its adherents the practice of a magic distinctly black. In Anglesey the Romans' usual tolerance of native cults was supended and, says Tacitus, 'the religious groves, dedicated to superstition and barbarous rites, were levelled to the ground. In those recesses the natives smeared their altars with the blood of their prisoners and in the entrails of men explored the will of the gods.'

THE VOTIVE HOARD
OF LLYN CERRIG BACH

Posidonius, a contemporary of Caesar who travelled widely in Gaul, wrote of both 'sacred precincts' and 'sacred pools' (or 'marshes'). Llyn Cerrig Bach, near Cymyran Bay on Anglesey, must have been such a sanctuary where offerings were thrown from a rock shelf into the water. We have seen hints of such practices in the Bronze Age (page 47). In 1943 a mechanical scoop working on the construction of Valley airfield extracted from the peaty margin of the lake an astonishing array of Early Iron Age objects, together with bones of ponies, oxen, sheep and pigs. It was impossible to conduct systematic excavation in the urgency of wartime, and the site is now buried; the 138 objects catalogued (in the National Museum of Wales) are probably but a fraction of what still lies hidden. The list includes swords, scabbards and daggers, chariot wheels and fittings, gang chains for slaves, iron bars of the kind used in southern England as currency, tongs, bracelets, spears and their ash-wood shafts, decorative plaques and mountings of bronze, shields, horse bits, two cauldrons (both with riveted repair patches) and part of a trumpet. In 1943 one gang chain was being used for hauling lorries out of the sticky peat before its venerable age was recognized. In this hoard is more iron than has been found elsewhere in our region for the whole of the 'Iron Age' together. There is nothing in the collection made after about A.D. 60. Cauldrons, gang chains and harness come near this date. Some weapons and bits may be 200 years earlier, and the rest falls within these dates. In A.D. 61 the Roman army under Suetonius Paulinus wiped out Druidism in Anglesey.

A POSSIBLE REASON
FOR THE LLYN CERRIG BACH HOARD

Some of the objects from Llyn Cerrig Bach were made elsewhere than in Anglesey itself: the long narrow tube and mouthpiece of a trumpet and one horse bit in Ireland; the gang chains and some harness fittings in eastern or south-eastern England where the Iron Age C Belgae, with their European connexions and well-known slave trade, were dominant; and the currency bars and other bronze fittings round the Severn mouth. The 'foreignness' of some of the items of bronze work can be disputed, and the more homely articles were surely not brought from far. Blacksmiths' tongs and a sickle surely betoken local activities; such things are indeed less to be expected as offerings. At least a part of the collection could be the result of the terrible defeat by the Romans in A.D. 61: a final jettisoning of property, perhaps an attempt to propitiate the irate gods, before refugee ships set sail for Ireland or farther north.

THE TAL Y LLYN HOARD

Another example of fine bronze craft has recently come to light. Eighteen pieces of bronze were found together in 1963, lying beneath a large boulder on very steep ground on the slope of Ystrad Gwyn, a southern flank of Cader Idris. Several of the pieces with triskele patterns came off a shield (fig. 41, page 55). Disks perforated with triskele patterns may have decorated a chariot or waggon. The openwork design on the disks is in typical curling Celtic style, like a splendid plaque in the Llyn Cerrig Bach hoard.

Close study of the method of engraving these mounts inclines some authorities to consider the possibility of an independent North Welsh school of bronzesmiths, continuing direct from the Late Bronze Age and receiving as always new inspiration by the western seaways. On this view the new con- tinental styles are thought to be introduced as early as the third and second centuries. Others see these objects, and many of those from Llyn Cerrig Bach, as imports made by craftsmen trained in Yorkshire, the Thames valley or round the Severn mouth, whose work, or who themselves, followed their clients —adventurers, refugees or pious pilgrims on their way to Anglesey—into Wales during the last century B.C.

CHARIOTS

Some of the most humdrum-looking objects at Llyn Cerrig Bach were strips of iron, but they proved to be among the most interesting. They are pieces of the steel tyres of at least ten, possibly as many as twenty-two war chariots, some almost new, some much worn. The National Museum has a model of what a war chariot might have looked like (fig. 44), combining the evidence of these and other

Fig. 44 *Model of a war chariot, suggested by finds among the Llyn Cerrig Bach hoard. The ponies would wear collars with traces and pull on the yoke as well. The side screens are of wickerwork with decorated bronze strips along the top. The pole is of cherry or hawthorn wood, joined to the yoke by an iron pin and strengthened with rivetted iron strips on either side. The hand holds have decorated bronze knobs. (Courtesy National Museum of Wales. Reconstruction by Sir Cyril Fox)*

finds, and comparing it with what is said in classical and Irish literature. Two ponies of 12 hands or less drew the warrior with his spears and sword, and the charioteer, both standing on the small, yard-square platform. The wheels, like the spear shafts, were of ash wood, and bent round into a circle. The tyres have no nail holes, and must therefore have been shrunk on to each wheel when hot, tightly compressing it when cold and making it strong and springy. The warrior could run out along the shaft pole and jump off and on to the platform by holding the bronze-capped 'horns'. The chariot was so manageable that it could be turned at full gallop on a steep slope. Chariot fighting had long since gone out of use among the European Celts, and Caesar and Tacitus both write of the dismay of the Roman soldiers when they first had to withstand chariot attacks in Britain. The heap of chariots at Llyn Cerrig is a moving monument, both to the discipline and courage of the Roman soldiers who stood up to these tactics, and to the despair of the charioteers. There are other signs of defeat here, too: swords bent or broken, chariot fittings scarred, bridle bits distorted in a patently deliberate manner. We cannot tell whether this was an act of revenge by the Romans or the last sacrifice of the Druids.

ANIMAL HEADS IN CELTIC ART

A consistent style runs through all Celtic design (figs. 38, 39, 40). With a combination of fantasy and observation, the pattern of plant growth is followed, though the result is remote from the leaves and stalks from which it began. The treatment of animals is similar. The most popular animal is the ox; little ox heads often adorn bowls and caul-

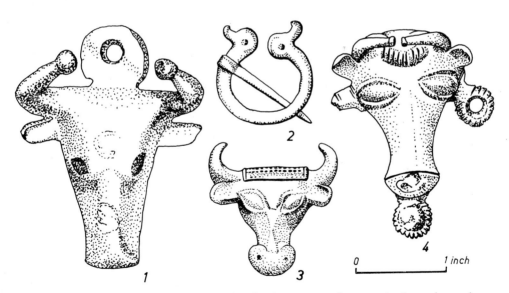

Fig. 45 *Animals in Celtic Art. 1 Dinorben, third or fourth century* A.D. *bronze ox-head escutcheon, 2 bronze duck-headed brooch from Llanferres, late first century* B.C.–*early first century* A.D., *3 bronze ox-head escutcheon, first–second century* A.D., *Dinorben, 4 bronze ox-head escutcheon, first–second century* A.D., *Welshpool*

drons. Two were found in excavations at Dinorben, one on the road built soon after the Roman attack (fig. 45.3). This charming beast is full of life in spite of the use of stylized Celtic patterns for its outlines and eyes.

The ox head was used on an elaborate iron fire-dog, sent with its owner to furnish his abode in the next world, and found buried

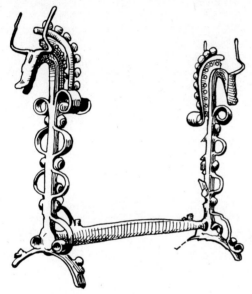

Fig. 46 *The Capel Garmon fire-dog, found lying on its side, a large stone at each end, in a peat bog at Carreg Goediog. Height 2 ft. 5½ in., length 3 ft. 6 in. from nose to nose*

in a cist at Capel Garmon. This is a splendid piece of fantasy (fig. 46) with ox heads whose arched, horse-like necks are adorned with helmet crests looking like horses' manes, possibly a stylized view of the bull bedecked for sacrifice. The great loops of iron ribbon were to hold bars or spits.

The little duck brooch from a burial cave at Llanferres is another example of Iron Age animals.

A BELGIC BURIAL AT WELSHPOOL

Another Celtic ox head (fig. 45.4) was among the treasure buried at Welshpool with a rich chieftain, whose family seems to have left eastern England during the troubles of the Roman invasion and settled in Cornovian territory where collaboration with the conqueror was considered wiser than resistance. The date of the burial is about A.D. 150, but the burial is in Celtic tradition. The chieftain was given for the next world what he would need to feast his companions in fit style. He owned both Roman and native metalwork. Italian and Gaulish wine jugs and handled pans of bronze were carefully wrapped in fine linen and packed with hay and dry leaves into a large cauldron to which this ox head had been attached. His tankard was like the Trawsfynydd one, of yew wood mounted with bronze. Firedogs, a tall lampholder of iron, glass jars and pottery completed the equipment.

8 The Romans

The Roman occupation gave our region three centuries of foreign rule. The soldiers built forts, and roads to connect them. They supervized the exploitation of mines and kept the peace. The impression of their presence is that of an occupying army, not of civilizing colonists. The great contribution of the Romans to Britain was the introduction of towns, with fine stone-built public buildings and spacious private houses, with central heating and drainage, baths, theatres and temples. After their defeat, the Silures in South Wales were encouraged to develop their tribal centre at Caerwent into such a town. There is no such town in North Wales. Gracious living, with imported wine, oil, fine pottery and glass, so noticeable in the Lowlands in towns and country villas alike, did not penetrate to our region. The army doubtless provided customers. Booths, taverns, oyster bars, for example, grew up round the forts, a little money and a few valuables were acquired for services to the soldiery, slaves and recruits were drawn from the local population, but life continued much as before.

SUBJUGATION
OF THE ORDOVICES

In A.D. 61 Suetonius Paulinus marched his troops into Snowdonia, built flat-bottomed transport boats to carry the infantry, put the auxiliary cavalry to swim across the straits, and defeated the native forces in Anglesey. Local tradition tells that he operated a pincer movement and sent some troops round to the west coast by water to land at Porth Swtan, which bears his name. Archaeology has not so far confirmed this. The revolt of Boudicca in south-east England necessitated his rapid withdrawal into England and full occupation of North Wales was the work of Agricola. He was appointed governor at the end of the summer in A.D. 78. The Ordovices had just wiped out a cavalry detachment sent from Viroconium (Wroxeter) or Chester to forage in their territory. Knowing the region from his service there under Suetonius Paulinus, he immediately set out to subdue the Ordovices and, according to Tacitus, 'completely destroyed the Ordovician State'. He pressed on. His cavalry was a select band chosen from local recruits who knew the terrain and were 'hardened to the national practice of swimming across lakes and rivers with dexterity'. He set the cavalry to ford the Straits, without waiting for supporting transport. The defenders, dumbfounded, surrendered the island. The cornfields and copper mines of Môn, Mam Cymru, belonged to the Romans.

The Deceangli had been conquered earlier. Ostorius Scapula overran their territory even before the defeat of Caratacus in A.D. 51. They probably decided that more was to be gained by collaborating with the Romans than joining the wild Ordovicians in their guerrilla warfare against the advancing legions. The defeat of Caratacus in 51, the massacre of the Druids in 61 and the final defeat by Agricola in 78, confirmed this belief. A 'pig' of lead stamped DECEANGL and dated A.D. 74 shows that the tribe was by then already peacefully working the Flintshire lead-mines for the Government.

PACIFICATION AND CONSOLIDATION

Agricola now ordered construction of the first fort at Segontium (Caernarfon). It was connected by road with the legionary base at Chester and with other forts distributed to hold the whole of Snowdonia: Kanovium (Caerhun), Bryn y Gefeiliau, Caer Gai, Tomen y Mur, Llystyn. The region was under the command of a legion, composed mainly of Roman citizens, stationed at the base fortress at Chester, while the advanced forts were manned by auxiliary troops, recruited or conscripted from among the subject peoples of the Empire. A few stamped tiles and inscribed

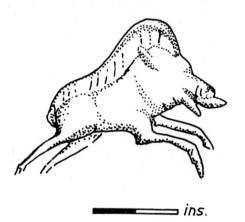

ins.

Fig. 47 *The boar, insignia of the XX Legion, Valeria Victrix, stamped on a tile made at the legionary pottery works at Holt while the Legion was based on Chester and controlled North Wales. After subduing North Wales, the legion did much service on the Wall in North Britain, while keeping Chester as its H.Q.*

stones give clues to the origins of the auxiliaries. It was, for obvious reasons of discipline, normal practice to use these troops in countries away from their homelands. The first cohort of Sunici from near Cologne was garrisoned at Segontium around A.D. 200, and

was earlier working at the legion's pottery works at Holt. Caer Gai was manned early in the second century by the first cohort of Nervii who came from Belgic Gaul. Inscriptions on altars and tombstones show that the legionaries stationed at Chester came from many parts of central Europe, Italy, Greece, Spain, and even from Syria and the Euphrates. A legion was 6,000 men strong, all heavy armed infantry except for 120 mounted dispatch riders, and was divided into ten cohorts; the auxiliaries were either infantry, cavalry, or a mixed force of both. The Sunici were probably a mixed cohort, 500 strong. The Nervii were 500 infantry.

THE ROAD NETWORK

Roads were the lifeline of the army, and as soon as a region was occupied, road building began (see frontispiece map). Captives and conscripts would be set to work under army supervision. From the base at Chester a road ran to Segontium. Not all of it can now be located, but a third-century Roman road book, the 'Antonine Itinerary', gives a list of roads and places along them, with distances, and this is a help to tracing it. It passed a small fort at Prestatyn. Parts of this, including a bath-house, were excavated in 1936, about half a mile S.S.W. of the parish church, but are no longer visible. Here much pottery, window glass and animal bones were found. The road went to the fort at Kanovium, one of the first to be built, passing a site called Varae which is still undiscovered, but likely to be near Rhuddlan. Beyond Kanovium the ditches on either side of the Roman road are clearly to be seen. It runs across the moor between Ro Wen and the coast west of Llanfairfechan, using for a stretch the old Bronze Age trackway through Bwlch y Ddeufaen. Near Rhiwiau two milestones have been found, corresponding to two periods of road building. They are now in the British

Museum. One dates from A.D. 121, when the Emperor Hadrian was in Britain consolidating the occupation of North Wales, before his work in the north, building the Wall against the Scottish tribes. The milestone records the eighth Roman mile from Kanovium (fig. 48). The second was set up about A.D. 208 in the time of Septimius Severus, who was also reorganizing the army in Wales. Another early milestone has been found, near Dinorwig camp, of the time of Trajan, and one from Gwaenysgor was set up in the time of Severus Alexander, between 231 and 235. Another road from Chester passed the legionary pottery works at Holt, established to supply the fort at Chester with tiles, drainpipes and pottery for the mess. Rows of kilns and workmen's barrack blocks were excavated, storehouses, a bath-house and the director's house with its central heating. Nothing can be seen there now, but the lane down to the river is still red with trodden pottery and bricks, and fragments of tiles and pipes fill the ploughed fields around.

The road went through Ffridd and then ran up or parallel to the Dee valley to Caer Gai on Bala Lake. From here one branch passed a signalling station, recently discovered above Pont Rhyd y Sarn, on its way to Brithdir. The road can be seen running higher up the valley to the south of the modern main road. Beyond Brithdir it joined the road called Sarn Elen, which linked Kanovium through Tomen y Mur with Pennal, itself linked with Llanio in Cardiganshire. A second branch from Caer Gai ran to Tomen y Mur, in part along the earlier trackway to Llanbedr (see p. 48). Beyond Moel y Slatus lies a group of practice camps, built by training contingents from Tomen y Mur. The road between Kanovium and Tomen y Mur (perhaps the bleakest fort the army had to man) took several slightly different courses at different periods. One went through Bryn y Gefeiliau on the Llugwy, where a large fort was discovered not many years ago. The road to Segontium took in Tremadoc and Llystyn, and there were more direct links through the Snowdon passes, past a station at Pen y Gwryd.

Fig. 48 *Roman milestone found at Rhiwiau Uchaf, Llanfairfechan, nearly 7 miles west of Kanovium. The inscription reads:*

IMP CAER TRAI/ANUS HADRIANUS/AUG·P·M·TR·P/ P·P·COS·III·/ A KANOVIO M·P·VIII

(*The Emperor Caesar Trajan Hadrian Augustus, Pontifex Maximus, with Tribunician Power, Father of his Country, three times Consul. From Kanovium, 8 miles (this would be along the road over the mountain). This milestone is carefully shaped and lettered. Later ones are much rougher. (Courtesy, British Museum)*

TREMADOC

At Tremadoc the southward road from Segontium came to a ferry or ford. A bath-house was built here. It had plastered and coloured walls, a heating system of tiled flues and hypocausts (a furnace under the floor sent hot air round cavities in floor and walls), flagged or concrete floors and underground drainage. Lavatories with running water were included in every permanent Roman build-ing, an amenity forgotten for many centuries after the Romans left. Pottery of the second to fourth centuries, a shale bracelet, black-smith's tongs and lead piping were among the finds. It has not been discovered to what kind of institution this bath was attached, whether civil or military. It was perhaps a posting house or inn. Bathing for the Romans was a lengthy affair and an important part of life. It included plunges in hot and cold water, sitting in different rooms (some for steam, some for dry heat to cause sweating), then massage, oiling, scraping the skin and a final cold plunge. It was a social function for all ranks and callings.

THE MINES

Roman military sites are often found near mineral deposits. The site at Prestatyn, where the inlet was then navigable, dominated the lead-mines at Meliden and Talar Goch. Wooden pumps and a shovel of oak were left by Romans mining at Tre' Castell Henryd, north of Kanovium. Lead was one of the principal sources of silver and the lead of Flintshire is especially rich in silver. Much of this was used for coinage, and hoards of silver coin found near Llandudno were per-haps destined to pay the copper-miners on the Great Orme. In the mines themselves, here and on Parys Mountain, Roman hammers and other tools, pottery and occasional coins have been found. C. Nipius Ascanius was a first-century Roman contractor whose name appears on lead 'pigs' from various sources, Flintshire among them. The lead from Halkyn Mountain was smelted at Pentre, with Flint-shire coal. The workers' dwellings, and a supervisor's house, have been encountered in excavations. These lead deposits may have been already worked in the Iron Age.

Lead was probably also worked near Llan-gynog. A large hill-top settlement lies on Craig Rhiwarth above the valley.

Roman copper-mines are known at Aber-ffraw, Pengarnedd, and Abergele as well as on Parys Mountain and the Great Orme. Several sources on Pumlumon were exploited; no doubt many other mines remain to be discovered. Great cakes of smelted copper, 30 to 50 lb in weight, have been found on Anglesey from time to time. They all lay near mines or native villages, and smelting and casting were carried out in some of the huts excavated. On the Great Orme, on the other hand, the miners lived close by the mines and, whether slaves or labourers, had no craftsmen among them. The small huts and cave dwellings give a picture of poor living. Shellfish were eaten in quantity, the shells were then used for paving the floors. A few terraces show they had some crops. Copper cakes found in Caernarfonshire include several stamped with the names of private companies under contract to the army. Two found on the beach at Llanystumdwy suggest a loading casualty; two on Carnedd Llywelyn are perhaps a clue to an unlocated mine nearby, for this is an unlikely place for a smithy, or a trading post.

SEGONTIUM

Segontium is the most important and best-excavated fort in our region. Its different stages are a guide to the history of the whole region under its sway. It is typically Roman in layout. The area of about $5\frac{1}{2}$ acres was surrounded by two W-shaped ditches each

6 feet deep and 7 feet wide. A wooden palisade stood in front of the earthen banks. Towers stood at each corner, a road ran all round inside the defences and there was a gateway in each side with square guard towers and a heavy double door. A road cut the long axis into two unequal halves. This was the *Via Principalis*, and the main buildings gave on to it: the *Principia*, or headquarters, and the residence of the commanding officer. From headquarters another road, the *Via Praetoria* (General's Street) ran to the gate in the front wall, the *Porta Praetoria*. On either side of this road stood barracks. Behind the central buildings ran another road, the *Via Quintana* (of the fifth cohort) and behind this again, divided by a *Via Decumana* (of the tenth cohort, farthest from the enemy) lay barracks, stables and storehouses (*retentura*), raised granaries with rows of wooden bins. Bath-houses and the huts of camp followers and native traders lay outside the defences, mainly along the roads leading to the gate.

The headquarters building at Segontium was arranged round a pleasant open court-yard, enclosed by a veranda and with a well near the centre. Behind the courtyard was a hall, and behind the hall the central shrine with the Emperor's statue and regimental standards, with offices on either side. When the garrison was reduced and the fort strengthened, in the mid-second century, stone replaced timber and a stone colonnade, partly closed in, took the place of the veranda. Red sandstone from Cheshire was used both here and at Kanovium, which was also built in stone at this time.

The close of the second century saw insurrection in the army and civil war within the Empire. Segontium was neglected as the troops went abroad to support their Governor, Albinus, in his bid for the Imperial throne. He was defeated, and his successful rival, Septimius Severus, came to Britain in about 208 to put a wasted province in order. In uncertain times like these people hid their wealth, and buried their savings.

COIN HOARDS

Before all was secure at the end of the first century a set of bronze saucepans holding Roman money was deposited for hiding at Ynys Gwrtheyrn near Harlech. The continued or renewed wealth of this populous area since the Bronze Age is shown again in the burial of a Celtic lady at Llechwedd Du with a fine bronze platter and mirror. Another coin hoard of this period has been found at Llanfaethlu on Anglesey. Insecurity before the reoccupation of Segontium under Septimius is reflected in a hoard of coins collected between 69 and 192 and deposited at Pentir, Caernarvonshire. Another hoard found in the bed of a stream near Llanfairfechan consisted entirely of silver coins, with dates ranging over 300 years. Most of them were minted in the time of Septimius.

THE RE-OCCUPATION OF SEGONTIUM

Much rebuilding went on about 210. There are signs of neglect and extensive fire before the reconstruction. The aqueduct supplying water to the fort was repaired by a cohort of the Sunici, who recorded the work in an inscription on stone. Both the north-east and south-west gates were rebuilt. Towers were added at the north-east gate and on the northern corner, with catapult platforms. Inside, the offices were re-equipped and central heating was installed in the quarter-master's office and his walls decorated with painted plaster. An altar to Minerva, Goddess of Wisdom, was installed in his apartments. The hall was divided into separate rooms, probably offices, and a strong-room established for the treasury. In earlier times, to avoid risk of fire, baths were built outside the fort. Now a new bath-house was built inside, for staff only. In short, the administrative side had grown in importance: bureaucrats instead of soldiers were in charge.

Outside the fort a large civil settlement grew up, much of it now under the modern town. Wharves and quays by the water's edge were busy with the merchant fleet and the navy. A temple of Mithras has lately been excavated near the fort. It was a small shrine, with a porch and nave flanked by benches ending in an alcove for an image. During the third-century occupation a few officers evidently practised this highly serious and ascetic cult of the Persian fire-god. Late in the fourth century some angry Christians penetrated the deserted shrine and desecrated it. The end of the third and early fourth century is again a time of coin hoards: finds include three hoards on Anglesey (at Llanidan, Trearddur Farm on Holyhead, and Din Silwy). A hoard at Llandwrog consisted of coins minted between 270 and 273. The most numerous, and the largest, hoards, were hidden during the first half of the fourth century. Prosperity had grown among the population during the century of peace. A few soldiers perhaps settled on retirement among the hills they had grown to love. Four fourth-century hoards have been found buried in pots in Denbighshire, besides two in the hill-fort of Moel Fenlli itself, two more in Anglesey, and a number in the ever-prosperous Flintshire.

At the turn of the century North Wales was thrown on its own resources. Segontium was empty for about fifty years. Troops were more urgently needed to defend the east and south of England against the Saxon invaders. But meanwhile the tempo of arrival of unwelcome settlers from Ireland, and of piratical raids, was increasing on the coasts. Resistance to these, in the absence of the Roman army, must have been centred on the hill-forts, many of which were comparatively flourishing hill-top towns during the fourth century, continuing the traditional Celtic way of life.

THE HILL-FORTS

The hill-forts known from excavation were nearly all occupied at this period, and we can assume that others were also occupied. A vivid impression of the layout of such a town can be gained from *Tre'r Ceiri*, where the huts, many levelled down into the scree, are unusually well preserved (fig. 42). The contrast with a Roman town, planned much like a fort, is striking; no central planning authority was at work here. The wall-walk and parapet on the surrounding wall, found also at Caer y Twr (Anglesey), Pen y Corddyn and Caer Drewyn, hint, however, at Roman ideas of defence. The huts were not richly furnished. In them was found pottery made during the second, third and fourth centuries, iron implements including a bill-hook, Roman beads. More decorative and valuable is a late first century A.D. gold-plated bronze brooch with Celtic designs, and parts of a gold-plated bronze necklace. Not a single quern has been found on Tre'r Ceiri. This suggests it was the summer resort of the occupants of the stone huts in the valley below. Warfare, cattle raiding and piracy were wholly summer pursuits, coinciding with summer pasturage. Meat and milk were presumably the upland diet. Baking was done in winter.

Surface finds of coins, a ring and pottery at *Dinas Dinlle* show second- and third-century occupation. On *Din Silwy* coins have been found ranging from Nero (54–68) to Constantius (292–306). *Braich y Dinas*, a large and busy hill-town, has been completely removed by quarrying on Penmaenmawr. Its stone huts were inhabited between A.D. 100 and 400. Roman pottery found its way there, and a silver snake bracelet. Spindle whorls and querns of both saddle and rotary type were used by the women in their work. At *Dinorben* the scatter of objects gives an unbroken sequence from the second century onwards in the shape of animal bones, coins, ploughshares, and broken coarse pottery which littered the huts and ground. The sporadic huts of crofters, built over the slighted defences of the Iron Age fort, were buried under a mighty rampart during the Roman period, which in the third century A.D. was enlarged and given an even wider military ditch outside it. The main entrance was made increasingly secure with added heavy doors placed at intervals along the long narrow passage through the thickened or inturned wall. This plan was used also at Tre'r Ceiri, Moel Fenlli and Caer y Twr. There were also square guard-houses at the inner end of the entrance passage, like Caer Drewyn and Pen y Corddyn. The fourth-century level gives the first indication that there were differences of status or wealth among the inhabitants: the large circular house of a chieftain lies to the north of the fort; his retainers were housed in small huts round the southern entrance. Dinorben seems to have been a permanent town, like Braich y Dinas.

FARMS AND VILLAGES

We have mentioned already (Chapter 6) the 'enclosed hut groups' with their cultivation terraces. Excavations at Rhostryfan, near Gaerwen, in a rectangular enclosure revealed both round and oblong workshops of a smithy, with two forges and a number of hearths. There were iron nails, horseshoes and slag, glass beads, rough pottery, a silver ring and a fragment of decorated bronze. Roman pottery of the second to fourth centuries shows a little contact with the garrison, over the generations. At Cae'rmynydd, a farm near Dinorwig, a Roman pot was carefully riveted to mend a break. The alternative to pottery, a bowl made of oak wood, was by

rare chance preserved among charcoal in a hut excavated at Cors y Gedol. Drains under the floors here show an awareness of Roman plumbing techniques. Locally-made hard black, and coarser pink, ware is found, in small quantities, in most of the excavated huts.

DWELLINGS IN ANGLESEY

The huts in the large village on Holyhead Mountain, under the wing of Caer y Twr, frequently contain grinding-stones and copper and iron slag. There were bronze- and iron-workers among the villagers as well as the farmers whose terraces still survive. On Anglesey some inroads were made into the forested land of the interior during Roman times. Caer Leb is typical. It is an area with five straight sides surrounded by two banks and two ditches which were probably moats. A rectangular building against the inner bank and a circular hut with a paved floor in the centre contained a little Roman pottery of the third century, animal bones, iron agricultural tools, a bronze brooch and querns.

The splendidly preserved group of buildings at Din Llugwy is also surrounded by straight walls. It consists of both round and straight-sided buildings. Coins and pottery (many pots mended with iron rivets), show that it was inhabited mainly in the fourth century. Iron-working went on in one building and a bloomery floor was found a short distance outside the palace.

Although they are called Cyttiau'r Gwyddelod (Irishmen's huts), there seems no reason to think that all hut circles in North Wales were, in fact, built by Irish immigrants: enclosed homesteads with terraces are a distinctive type of settlement and thus were probably built by a distinct group of people, but their ancestry is not found in Ireland. As is often suggested, Din Llugwy is perhaps the stronghold of an Irish chieftain. A foreign origin for a site so unique in its design and spaciousness is possible—but Ireland was hardly 'foreign': the continuous contacts with Ireland since neolithic times explain why there is so little sign in archaeology of the Irish intruders who dominate the earliest written histories in Wales, and who must have been arriving during the last two centuries of Roman rule.

CONCENTRIC CIRCLES

About sixteen sites of a special type can be seen on the northern coast of Caernarfon and, even more frequently, in Ardudwy. Two of them are called Muriau'r Gwyddelod, but there is none in Anglesey, where the great final battle against the Irish took place during the fifth century, and where one would expect to find most traces of Irish settlements. They are round houses, surrounded by one or more rings of thick walls, inside which cattle could be herded. Often they are built over the ruins of enclosed homesteads, and have walls running from them enclosing large areas of cattle run. Whoever the new-comers were, they drove the earlier farmers off and used their cultivation terraces as platforms for their own houses and yards. They may have been a few families of Irish cattle farmers with special ideas of building, or they may be imagined as the homes of the followers of Cunedda. This legendary group of warriors came from the Firth of Forth after the departure of the Romans and ejected the Irish, setting up the long dynasty of Gwynedd.

THE LAST MANNING OF SEGONTIUM

Raids from Picts and Scots on the north and west frontiers of the Empire became as serious as Saxon raids in the east and south of Britain. In the middle of the fourth century legionary troops returned to occupy Segontium in strength. The fort was repaired and Caer Gybi on Holyhead was built to withstand the threat from across the sea. Caer Gybi is a small rectangular enclosure with solid circular towers, and a lower wall forming a quay, similar in construction to the Saxon shore defences of the east.

Meanwhile, at the centre, the Roman Empire was crumbling. The raids on England and Wales were echoes of barbarian attacks on the heart of the Empire itself, and the spirit to withstand them was not there. Civil war and dissension were rife. In 383 Magnus Maximus, a native of Spain and Governor of Britain, led off his troops to Gaul to support his claim to be Emperor. There is nothing to show they ever returned. They left behind them in Wales a growing legend of a splendid city, its streets paved with gold, the abode of Helen, mother of Constantine, whom Maxen Wledig saw in a dream and came from Rome to marry. She symbolizes perhaps the lure of the gold-bearing Celtic West, the Roman dream of world empire. The name of this mythical Helen of the Legions, daughter of a Welsh chieftain and wife of Magnus Maximus, is enshrined in the road, Sarn Elen, whose builders now departed, as foreign as they had come.

They left a Celtic land behind. Legends of Vortigern, Arthur and Merlin took possession of the mountains with the hill-fort of Dinas Emrys in its heart.

The bards sang of Welsh heroes and heroines: of Branwen, Aranrhod, and Pryderi in Aberffraw and Harlech. But from Ireland once again came new and fertile inspiration. It is touching to visit Caer Gybi and see the Roman coastguard's fort surrounding the church of a Celtic saint who came from Ireland to preach the gospel. The debt of the Irish raids was repaid, soon after the Romans had gone, by the civilizing missions of Irish Christians.

Gazetteer of Sites

ANGLESEY

BARCLODIAD Y GAWRES

CHAMBER TOMB
DATE: Neolithic or Early Bronze Age
MAP REF.: 328708
DIRECTIONS: 1-inch O.S. map. A track leads from the road at Porth Trecastell to the site at the end of the promontory. Official guide pamphlet.

A recently excavated passage grave with cruciform chamber restored according to the most modern ideas, combining visibility with the genuine effect. Five of the stones are carved with Iberian-type patterns, the best example of tomb art so far discovered in the British Isles outside Ireland.

Powell and Daniel, *Barclodiad y Gawres*, 1956

BRYN CELLI DDU

CHAMBER TOMB
DATE: Neolithic or Early Bronze Age
MAP REF.: 508702
DIRECTIONS: 1-inch O.S. map. Track leads to farm, where the key is kept. Entrance fee, 3*d*. Official guide pamphlet, with plan, 3*d*.

The passage grave, surrounded by a ditch and four stone circles, with entrance forecourt to the east, was originally covered by a round mound 160 feet in diameter. Most of the mound had disappeared by 1928, when it was excavated. A mound now covers only the inner passage and chamber to protect it, leaving the ditch and circles visible. The carved stone found at the centre of the circles, just outside the chamber, is now in the National Museum, but a cast replaces it on the site. Note portal where the covered passage begins, the bench along north wall of this passage, and pillar stone inside the chamber.

About 500 yards north-west of the site is a standing stone, 10 feet high; 180 yards south-west is a smaller standing stone. A tumulus containing a small cist was excavated 40 yards south-south-west. There is little now to be seen of the kerb and ditch. Two Graig Lwyd axes, and a bronze palstave have been found near the farm.

Archaeologia, 83

BRYN YR HEN BOBL AND PLAS NEWYDD

CHAMBER TOMBS
DATE: Neolithic; *c*. 2800 B.C.
MAP REF.: 518690, 520697
DIRECTIONS: 1-inch O.S. map. Plas Newydd cromlech stands right in front of the mansion. Permission should be sought from the estate agent of the Marquess of Anglesey before visiting.

Plas Newydd may possibly have been a passage grave, with the passage at the south leading into the polygonal chamber. The capstone is 11 feet 6 inches by 9 feet 6 inches by 3 feet 6 inches thick, and is held by five orthostats.

Bryn yr Hen Bobl lies half a mile to the south. The crescent-shaped cairn does not cover the small rectangular chamber, but curves round it, forming a large forecourt. It covers a complicated system of stone walls built behind the chamber. The lintel stone has two semicircular notches in the top edge, reminiscent of the 'portholes' found in the 'door' stone of megalithic tombs in many areas of the world. The forecourt was covered with charcoal patches from fires. At a later time it had been filled with stones to block the east-facing chamber. Among the stones was mixed a dark soil containing charcoal, pottery fragments, shells, broken stone tools and bones.

Archaeologia, 80
Tr. Anglesey Arch. Soc., 1953

CASTELL BRYN GWYN

CIRCULAR EARTHWORK
DATE: possibly Neolithic
MAP REF.: 466671
DIRECTIONS: 1-inch O.S. map

An area 200 feet in diameter is enclosed by a bank 10 feet high, the rest of its height now being spread over the enclosed area. Excavations showed that the defences had been remade several times, and deep ditches dug, which are not now visible. Finds were very few: they suggest the site might be late neolithic in origin, have continued in use during the Bronze Age, and been rebuilt during the Early Iron Age. About 300 yards north is the remains of a stone circle, diameter about 40 feet. Only two large stones are now standing. Faint traces of a ditch with an outer bank surround it. This is the only stone circle known in Anglesey.

Arch. Camb., 1962

BWRDD ARTHUR, OR DIN SYLWY

HILL-FORT

DATE: possibly Iron Age; certainly first to fourth century A.D.
MAP REF.: 586816
DIRECTIONS: 1-inch O.S. map

The hill-top is naturally defended by steep slopes on all sides. The 17 acres of almost flat top were enclosed by a stone wall, 8 feet thick, built of two lines of slabs set on edge filled in between with rubble. The lower part can be traced all round the site. Main entrance on the south, approached by modern cart track. Small postern gateway to narrow ledge path on west. Traces of hut sites and a semicircular enclosure within the defences. Finds include coins from Nero to Constantius, coarse Roman pottery of third and fourth centuries A.D. and traditional native wares.

R.C.A.M. Anglesey: Llanfihangel Din Silwy

CAER GYBI

COASTAL FORT

DATE: fourth century A.D.
MAP REF.: 247826
DIRECTIONS: In Holyhead town, enclosing St Cybi's church and churchyard.

The fort stands on a low cliff now in part built over, but the remains of the walls of the rectangular enclosure and its four corner towers are still impressive. The original wall is almost intact on north, west and south. The north-west tower remains in part up to the level of the wall walk. The north-east tower has been rebuilt in modern times, the lower 12 feet are original. There was a Roman wall running eastwards to enclose a quay. Defence was necessary at this time against Irish raids.

R.C.A.M. Anglesey: Holyhead Urban

CAER LEB

ENCLOSED SETTLEMENT

DATE: Third century A.D.
MAP REF.: 473674
DIRECTIONS: 1-inch O.S. map. In field beside the road.

Two banks and two ditches, holding water, enclosed a five-sided area 200 feet by 160 feet.

The outer ditch is now almost invisible. The banks were faced with stone. The entrance on the south was apparently a simple break in the banks. Other 'entrances' are modern, probably made by cattle. Like other less well-preserved enclosures in the then forested low-lying interior of Anglesey, it contains hut foundations similar to those of the settlements on the limestone hills, and was probably occupied by farmers who did not need the security of hill-forts, now that the Romans ensured peace, and were prepared to tackle forest clearance, perhaps doing a trade in timber. The ditches would drain water from the village and keep out wild animals, and the site was better hidden from Irish raiders than those by the coast.

R.C.A.M. Anglesey: Llanidan

CAER Y TWR, AND TY MAWR HUT GROUP

WALLED HILLTOP TOWN AND UNDEFENDED SETTLEMENT

DATE: second century A.D. onwards
MAP REF.: 218830
DIRECTIONS: Top of Holyhead mountain.

As at Din Silwy, a wall crowns the hill-top, enclosing about 17 acres. The interior is very rough and rocky, and there is no trace of hut foundations. There are terraces outside on the north-west. The entrance is in the north-east corner. The north side is best preserved, showing the 13 feet wide rampart, 19 feet high, with a wall walk 4 feet wide at a height of about a yard off ground. Three-quarters of a mile to the south-west is a large group of hut foundations, near Ty Mawr. Many have been destroyed by modern cultivation, but there still remain about twenty, and some cultivation terraces nearby. The inhabitants may have built the walls of Caer y Twr for a refuge against Irish raids, but never needed to build houses inside. In the village outside there are both round and oblong buildings, mostly with central hearths. Many contained hammer stones, mortars, querns, whetstones and spindle whorls, and coarse pottery. Copper slag and sand in two huts show that metal was worked.

R.C.A.M. Anglesey: Holyhead Rural

DIN DRYFOL

CHAMBER TOMB

DATE: early third millenium B.C.
MAP REF.: 395725
DIRECTIONS: 1-inch O.S. map. Best approached from the west, from Fferamdryfol Farm, Aberffraw, as the crossing of the stream

from the east, beyond that farmhouse, is rather a scramble.

A large side stone, 11 feet long, standing 5 feet high, has the 9 feet by 5 feet capstone resting on it. This is all that remains of what was probably a chamber with a portal. Thirty feet to the east another stone 10 feet high suggests that the tomb was a segmented cist at least 50 feet long. The site is unusual: the tomb nestles under the strange natural hump of the hillock called Dinas, built on a narrow terrace of rock above a valley.

Tr. of the Cymmrodorion Society, 1910–11

DIN LLUGWY

ENCLOSED SETTLEMENT
DATE: fourth century A.D.
MAP REF.: 496862
DIRECTIONS: A signpost shows the way from the road over a stile across two fields. The twelfth-century chapel lies to the right.

This is rightly the best known of walled hut groups. In shape and size it is comparable with Caer Leb, but there is much more to be seen. The entrance was through the rectangular building against the north-east wall. Iron was worked in the north-east corner building, four hearths for smelting had iron slag, ashes, etc, in the eastern part. A similar workshop was on the south wall. Outside this wall an enclosure was built up against it, divided from a second by a narrow space which seems to have been used as a rubbish dump by the hut users.

Pottery found in the huts was often mended by iron rivets, showing how it was prized. The pottery and coins together show that occupation was mainly in the fourth century. The tidy plan and splendid masonry suggest that this was rather a palace than native village. There are traces to show that it was built over an earlier undefended village.

A third of a mile west of the settlement is a smelting workshop where iron slag, charcoal and coal were found. Coal could be used to weld the blooms into iron bars such as were also found on the site, and are typical of Roman working.

About half a mile south-west of the settlement are three boiling mounds, two on the left, one on the right bank of the streamlet running into Afon Llugwy. The two on the left have been excavated, and contain hearths of stone and burnt clay. A well-used pounding-stone lay above one hearth. There was nothing to show the date of the mounds.

R.C.A.M. Anglesey: Penrhos Lligwy

LLUGWY CROMLECH

CHAMBER TOMB
DATE: early third millennium B.C.
MAP REF.: 501860
DIRECTIONS: 1-inch O.S. map

The 25-ton capstone, 18 feet by 15 feet by 3 feet 9 inches, rests on short megaliths standing over a natural cleft in the rock. The chamber is thus 6 feet deep. Its filling was excavated in 1908, with layers as follows: 2 feet top soil; 1 foot red clayey soil in and under which were many limpet shells, a deliberate sealing with remains of a feast; 15 inches of black soil ('occupation earth') and stones with human and animal bones, flint scrapers and fragments of pottery; a 3-inch paving of flat stones—another sealing; under this were 9 inches of black earth and small stones with more human bones and teeth and animal bones, including a piece made into a pin, flints and pottery, and many mussel shells in the lowest part. The human bones were broken or trampled into tiny pieces; at least thirty people had been buried in all, including one new-born child. Ox, sheep, pig, deer, fox, fowl, dog and otter bones were with them—a better feast than just limpets. Unfortunately no record was kept of possible differences between pottery above and below the paving-floor. It was mostly incised neolithic A ware, of the kind known from Beacharra in Scotland, but a few pieces decorated with shell are neolithic B.

Arch. Camb., 1933

PANT Y SAER

BURIAL CHAMBER
DATE: third millennium B.C.
MAP REF.: 510824
DIRECTIONS: 1-inch O.S. map

The uprights holding the broken capstone stand in a pit cut out of the solid rock. There is a complicated system of walls inside the oval mound, and some difference of opinion as to the right place for a forecourt seems to have been settled by making two, one where the mound curves inwards, where it is expected, and one in the western horn of the mound, cut into the rock and surrounded by a wall. The floor here showed signs of fires. There was much western neolithic pottery, and a cist burial had been inserted with a beaker. Neolithic burials included thirty-six adults, three adolescents, six children and nine unborn infants, even more overcrowding than at Llugwy. There were not enough skulls for all the long bones—a fact noticed in several other chambers outside

Wales. The pirate's emblem may be a very old one!

R.C.A.M. Anglesey: Llanfair M.E.
Arch. Camb., 1933
Daniel, *Prehistoric Chamber Tombs*, 1950, p. 91

TREFIGNATH

BURIAL CHAMBER
DATE: third millennium B.C.
MAP REF.: 259805
DIRECTIONS: 1-inch O.S. map

The gallery grave is 45 feet long. Two portal stones flank the easternmost chamber, 7 feet high. Many stones have been removed for gateposts in recent centuries, so that it now looks like three separate chambers. All traces of a mound have vanished in the last 100 years.

R.C.A.M. Anglesey: Holyhead Rural

TWYN Y PARC

PROMONTORY FORT
DATE: Iron Age; *c.* second to first century B.C.
MAP REF.: 370650
DIRECTIONS: 1-inch O.S. map

The defences are more elaborate than the earliest Iron Age ramparts. The earth and stone rampart which cuts off the neck of the promontory is protected by two banks which overlap the entrance and protect it. On the north-west side there is a wall to strengthen the defence of the cliff against attack from the creek, which made an excellent landing-place.

R.C.A.M. Anglesey: Llangadwaladr
(short description)

TY NEWYDD

BURIAL CHAMBER
DATE: Neolithic (?) and Early Bronze Age
MAP REF.: 344738
DIRECTIONS: 1-inch O.S. map

A classic 'cromlech'. In 1935 two stone pillars were built in to prevent widening of the crack in the capstone, and the floor was excavated. Black, charcoaly earth was found under a fallen wall stone, in it were mixed 110 pieces of broken white quartz, a common material in Bronze Age burials, a barbed and tanged Beaker-style arrowhead and fragments of pottery in two groups, almost certainly beakers. There was also a chip off a polished flint axe. Sections of walling suggested there had once been a passage, and this may have been the 'second chamber' mentioned in early descriptions. A fire, mostly of hazel wood, had been lit at the entrance to the chamber. There was no sign of any human bones. This is not enough evidence for saying that the tomb was built for the Beakers. If it was a passage grave, it might only have held cremations which were not uncovered.

There are very faint signs of a mound.

Arch. Camb., 1936

CAERNARVONSHIRE

BACHWEN, CLYNNOG CROMLECH

BURIAL CHAMBER
DATE: Neolithic
MAP REF.: 408495
DIRECTIONS: 1-inch O.S. map. A pleasant walk from Clynnog Fawr church leads to this sea-side site.

One of the best examples of cup-marks, on the capstone.

CAERAU

HUTS AND FIELD TERRACES, AND BOILING MOUNDS
DATE: second–fourth centuries A.D., mounds possibly earlier
MAP REF.: 470490, 464488
DIRECTIONS: On the Portmadoc-Caernarfon road, mostly on the straight stretch north of Caerau, to the east of the road, just over the wall and up the slope. The mounds, grass grown, are best reached past the farmhouse of Bodychain, on the west of the road, and down the track, avoiding the marsh.

There are both separate huts and enclosed farmstead groups, all connected with terraced fields of square Celtic shape, though some medieval strip lynchets cut across them. Excavation of enclosed group at 468489 showed there had been a central post in one room to hold up the roof, and a ring of posts in another. Each room had two hearths, one used for smelting iron, and there were elaborate drainage channels under the floor. Rotary querns, pieces of iron, perforated slate disks and second–third century A.D. pottery were found.

R.C.A.M. Caern. II: Clynnog

CONWY MOUNTAIN, CAER LLEION, OR CAER SEIONT

HILL-FORT
DATE: Iron Age; *c.* 350 B.C. onwards
MAP REF.: 760778
DIRECTIONS: 1-inch O.S. map

There is a single walled rampart all round, except on the north, where the hill is very steep. At the western end is a more strongly fortified enclosure, with outer bastions and ditches, apparently fortified as much against the larger enclosure as against the outside. There were several periods of building. About fifty-eight hut foundations can be seen. The entrance is narrow, through the thickened rampart on the south; a wooden bridge crossed above it. On its east side was a hut containing more than 400 sling stones. Other huts inside also contained sling stones. One had a hearth in the centre and near it a water-hole, and a saddle quern. No precise dating material was found.

R.C.A.M. Caern. I: Conway

DINLLAEN

PROMONTORY FORT
DATE: Iron Age: 100 B.C.
MAP REF.: 276418
DIRECTIONS: 1-inch O.S. map

This is the largest double-ramparted fort, the ramparts cut off a wide area of headland. Like Dinas Dinlle, it controls good harbourage. There are no traces of earlier occupation.

R.C.A.M. Caern. III

DINAS DINLLE

COASTAL HILL-FORT
DATE: Iron Age; 100 B.C.
MAP REF.: 437563

DIRECTIONS: 1-inch O.S. map. On the coast. One of the double, earth-ramparted forts built by the Iron Age B invaders about 100 B.C. Air photographs show that there were sheltered creeks, now submerged by the sea, controlled by the fort. The ramparts towards the sea have been destroyed by erosion, and the north-west corner is much altered by the golf course. Remains of huts along the eastern side. The entrance is a single gap on the south-east. The ditch between the ramparts is here protected by banks. Finds include coins of A.D. 253–96, a Roman finger ring and one small piece of pottery, which show occupation in the second and third centuries.

No traces of occupation before the Iron Age B ramparts.

R.C.A.M. Caern. II: Llandwrog

DINAS DINORWIG (sometimes called Caerau Dinas)

HILL-FORT
DATE: Iron Age; 400 B.C. onwards
MAP REF.: 550650

DIRECTIONS: 1-inch O.S. map. Close beside the road to Pentir from Llanrug.

The inner wall encloses a small 3-acre fort, with a large entrance at north-east and smaller at north-west. This belongs to the first period. Later, probably about 100 B.C., it was taken over by the Iron Age B invaders, who surrounded the walled fort with two massive earth ramparts faced with stone, blocking the larger north-east entrance, bringing a slanting track to the north-west wall entrance, protected by the curving ramparts. The modern farmhouse lies over the outer rampart, where it joined with the rampart of a northern annexe. The inside has been much cultivated, but one hut circle remains near the entrance. No signs of occupation in Roman period. The name perhaps means Dinas of the Ordovicians.

R.C.A.M. Caern. II: Llanddeiniolen
Arch. Camb., 1947

DINAS EMRYS

HILL-FORT
DATE: Early Iron Age to fifth century A.D.
MAP REF.: 606492
DIRECTIONS: 1-inch O.S. map. The easiest approach is from the east, following a track round to the north of the summit and approaching the site along the ridge.

The original entrance was from the west, a steep climb past three ramparts. Trees and later walls make it difficult to see the design of the defences, but the site has splendid command of the valley. The pool was artificially dug over earlier structures in the first century A.D. The sheltered hollow had been occupied by wooden buildings some centuries before that. A rough stone building of Roman date can be seen near the pool. The tower on the cliff above is twelfth century. Field terraces can be seen on all the slopes of the hill outside the defences, and a few hut circles. The pool is the spring where, in the medieval stories, the dragons prevented Vortigern from building his palace. Pottery, glass and iron slag show it was inhabited in the time of Vortigern.

R.C.A.M. Caern. II: Beddgelert
Arch. Camb., 1960

DRUIDS' CIRCLE, PENMAENMAWR

STONE CIRCLE
DATE: Bronze Age
MAP REF.: 723747
DIRECTIONS: 1-inch O.S. map. Road from Penmaenmawr to Bryn Derwydd.

77

An older trackway crosses to the north of the circle, which is slightly flattened to avoid it. It is only when approaching the circle from the east along this track that the circle is at all conspicuous from any distance. The stones vary much in size and distance from each other. All were set on the inner side of the bank of small stones. They are none of them of local rock, and were probably brought from the Snowdon area by glaciers. The surface was deliberately scattered with white quartz fragments. The entrance, much damaged by blasting to remove stones during the nineteenth century, is on the west. Excavation revealed a central cist carefully placed on direct line with the outlying stone and one of the tallest stones in the circle. The cist contained a large food vessel which held the cremation of a child of about 11. Four feet six inches west-north-west of this a similar urn was fitted into a pit just large enough to hold it. Cremated bones of a child about a year older than the central cremation were covered by it, and among the bones was a bronze knife. Eight feet south-east of the central cist was a small pit in which a broken food vessel had been placed upright with nothing in it. A trench led away from this pit for 2 feet 6 inches to the south-west, where it ended in a shallow hollow. This was lined with whetstones on which cremated bones, very crumbled, lay. A small circle 280 yards north-east of the Druids' Circle was excavated at the same time. All that was found was a thick scatter of quartz fragments and, 1 foot north of the centre, a small shallow pit crammed with quartz fragments. Other circles, cairns and hut circles abound on this moorland, particularly on the track that leaves south-westwards to join the Ro Wen-Aber track, and again round the top of the Aber valley.

The western half of the moorland has only Bronze Age and later remains. The eastern half was apparently occupied earlier, in neolithic times. Graig Lwyd lies just over the shoulder of the hill towards the coast from the Druids' Circle, and the Dinas and Garreg Fawr outcrops which were also used for axes lie to the south-west. Axes from these workshops have been found round Moel Lwyd and towards the Conwy valley.

Proceedings of the Prehistoric Society, 1960

LLANFAIRFECHAN

ARROW STONES, AND MOUNDS OF BURNT STONE
DATE: Bronze Age
GRID REF.: 695725
DIRECTIONS: Within half a mile of this grid reference can be found four arrow stones and four mounds of burnt stone, with five others not far away along the prehistoric trackway. These two classes are not necessarily related, but in a region full of round huts, cairns and near the Garreg Fawr axe workshop, which is likely to have been more habitable and populous during the Bronze Age than earlier or later.

Precise locations are:

arrow stones	mounds
69377229	68797288
69377228	68867217
69237238	68947232
69567315	69617299
	69617245

Near Bwlch y Ddeufaen
71067244
71187286
71547417
71757384

R.C.A.M. Caern. I: Llanfairfechan

LLETTY'R FILIAST, HWYLFA'R CEIRW, GREAT ORME

BURIAL CHAMBER; AVENUE OF STONES
DATE: Neolithic and Bronze Age
MAP REF.: 772830, 765840
DIRECTIONS: A little to the south, at the halfway stop of the tramway up the Great Orme, near disused shafts of copper-mines used certainly as early as Roman times.

The ruined five-sided chamber lies at the southeastern end of a long oval mound, partly natural, partly quarried away.

The avenue is composed of small stones, and leads north-north-east from the foot of a natural scarp to the top of a steep-sided hollow leading down to the sea. It is presumably of the same age and purpose as the avenue at Rhos y Beddau in Montgomeryshire (see p. 46).

R.C.A.M. Caern. I; Llandudno

LLYN PENINSULAR HILL-FORTS: GARN BODUAN; GARN FADRUN; PEN Y GAER, LLANAELHAEARN; CARN PENTYRCH, LLANGYBI

DATE: Iron Age; 400 B.C. onwards
MAP REF.: 314395, 280351, 429455, 425418
DIRECTIONS: O.S. map

There is not enough information to list these separately, and a visit to one of them is probably sufficient. Each dominates a hill-top, and was first built with one stone wall, probably at the arrival of Iron Age A invaders. Garn Boduan and Garn Fadrun were given a second, lesser defence like Caer Seiont, probably against Iron Age B invaders. All contain round huts, though at Pen y Gaer there are only platforms, no walls, and huts were probably of wood, except in two cases. At Garn Boduan sling stones were found in a hut near the ramparts, as at Conwy Mountain.

R.C.A.M. Caern. III
Arch. Camb., 1926

PEN Y GAER, LLANBEDR Y CENNIN

HILL-FORT
DATE: Iron Age; 400 B.C.
MAP REF.: 750693
DIRECTIONS: 1-inch O.S. map. Best approached from the north.

The entrance at the west is guarded by *chevaux de frise*—a setting of pointed stones. There are three defences with ditches and an outer ditch. The inner defence is a stone wall about 15 feet thick and is the earliest. The site may have been taken by Iron Age B invaders who put up their usual two earth ramparts. The *chevaux de frise* cannot be linked definitely to either period; it is a rare device in Britain and most of Europe, but is common in central Spain. It seems likely that the Iron Age B sea-invaders brought the idea. Levelled circular platforms inside are hut foundations. One contained traces of iron working. Two barrows north of the *chevaux de frise* were excavated. The old ground surface was covered with charcoal and burnt bone, with a few small fragments of copper and bronze. These may have been built early in the hill-fort's occupation, which, as usual, cannot be precisely dated by finds. It certainly was rebuilt at different times. The fields and long hut foundations to the south are probably medieval.

R.C.A.M. Caern. I Llanbedr y Cennin

RHOSTRYFAN, LLANWNDA

HUTS AND FIELDS
DATE: Iron Age and Roman; *c.* 100 B.C.–A.D. 400
MAP REF.: 505579   495573
          500582
          501585
DIRECTIONS: Some on 1-inch O.S. map. Hafoty Wern Las is a good centre to start from; the fields all round are full of hut foundations and field terraces, and standing stones mark field

boundaries. The blacksmith's workshop is on the right along the lane to Bod Angharad.

R.C.A.M. Caern. II: Llanwnda

RO WEN; MAEN Y BARDD, BWLCH Y DDEUFAEN; MAEN PENDDU AND CAER BACH

CROMLECH, STANDING STONES, HILL-FORT, AND ROMAN ROAD
DATE: Neolithic, Bronze Age, Iron Age and Roman; 3000 B.C.–A.D. 400
MAP REF.: 732715
DIRECTIONS: 1-inch O.S. map. The climb up from Ro Wen is so steep that many prefer to take the road past Hafoty Gwyn to Cae Coch. This joins the Roman road half-way between Bwlch y Ddeufaen and Maen y Bardd, beyond which the track climbs gently to Caer Bach and on to Maen Penddu.

The Roman road from Caerhun to Caernarvon, probably itself following an earlier trackway, is followed by a modern road as far as the mountain gate a quarter of a mile from the two standing stones marking the pass. Just before the gate, to the south over the wall, is a stone circle and a boiling mound. The ancient route continues across the moor as a well-marked track, and drops down to Aber as a modern road again. The Roman road leaves it earlier for the coast, past Rhiwiau Uchaf to Llanfairfechan. This was a populous district from Bronze Age times onwards; there are numerous cairns and hut circles, many not mapped. The Maen y Bardd cromlech is on the north of the road before the steep slope of Tal y Fan. It seems almost incredible that the Roman legions should have scaled the 1 in 3 hill direct to Ro Wen rather than going round by Hafoty Gwyn. Just before the road turns right past the Youth Hostel on its steep descent there is a stile leading up across fields to Caer Bach. This is a small hill-fort with two defensive rings; the outer is a bank of earth with ditch outside. A stone facing wall can be seen in places, and an extra bank to the south. The inner stone wall is dilapidated, and has been robbed. There is a hut circle against it on the north-west. Some rather ruined huts lie to the south-west, and some ruined cairns to the south. The track continues half a mile to Maen Penddu, a very large maenhir, where several tracks converge. One track continues across the moor to the Druids' Circle.

R.C.A.M. Caern. I: Llangelynin

SEGONTIUM

ROMAN FORT
DATE: A.D. 80–383
MAP REF.: 485624
DIRECTIONS: In Caernarfon, on the Beddgelert road. Admission at the Museum on the site,
adults 6*d*, children 3*d*. Reduced rates for parties of
eleven or more.

It is worth buying the 1*s* guide-book before visiting the foundations of the fort, and studying the
plan of the layout, so that the streets and buildings are clear. There are no visible traces of
the first, wooden buildings, but the rampart,
unchanged since the foundation of the fort, can
be seen along the north-east side, and the well in
the headquarters building III is from the early
period. Some wooden buildings were destroyed
by fire, and the first stone buildings were put up
about A.D. 150. Rebuilding took place about 210,
and again about A.D. 350.
  The Museum has an interesting and well-laid-
out collection of objects found during excavation,
and other finds.
R.C.A.M. Caern. II: Llanbeblig

TRE'R CEIRI

HILL-FORT
DATE: native town of Roman period A.D. 150–
400, perhaps earlier origin
MAP REF.: 373446
DIRECTIONS: 1-inch O.S. map. Approach by
track from the south up to the south-west entrance.

A splendid walled town. The track to the entrance
passes terraces and enclosures, for cattle or garden
plots. The main wall is best preserved on the north
and west, where the wall walk and parapet can be
seen. A second, outer wall to the north-west is
probably a later addition to the defences. The
large cairn at the top is presumably Bronze Age,
like so many other hill-top cairns. Sixty-nine of
the 150 huts have been excavated and produced
nothing dateable before A.D. 150. The earliest are
simple round huts. They were followed by round
huts divided by partitions, D-shaped huts placed
back to back, single D-shaped huts, and latest of
all long narrow huts, oval, many sided or nearly
rectangular. The foundations were levelled into the
scree covering the site, and the walls built up with
masonry from below ground-level, with the
entrance usually on the lower side.
  The town may well have started before the
Roman invasion and been one of the few to remain
occupied during the first two centuries of Roman

rule. Objects found are sparse, but prove occupation from A.D. 150 to about A.D. 400. No querns
were found, possibly because the fort was only
occupied in the summer, the season of warfare
and upland pasturage. In winter 'enclosed hut
groups' would be occupied, on land now mainly
inhabited and worked. The slopes coming down
to the little road running eastwards out of Llanaelhaearn to Cae'r wrach are covered with remains
of hut circles of every description, and field
terraces.
R.C.A.M. Caern. II: Llanaelhaearn

DENBIGHSHIRE

DINAS BRAN, LLANGOLLEN

HILL-FORT
DATE: second–first century B.C.; possibly
earlier origin
MAP REF.: 223430
DIRECTIONS: 1-inch O.S. map. Turn left past
the school, and then right at the cross-roads.

The medieval castle, reputed to have been built
by Gruffydd ap Madog ap Gruffydd Maelor in
1270, stands within the defences of an Iron Age
fort. On the west there is a rock-cut ditch inside
the rampart. In 1918 a bronze socketed axe was
discovered in the soil near the mouth of a rabbit-
hole on the south slope, 150 yards from the summit.
This is interesting as a sign that a Late Bronze
Age woodman, hunter or warrior was by the fort,
which may already have been built.

Ellis Davies, *Prehistoric and Roman Remains
of Denbighshire*, 1929, p. 252

CAPEL GARMON

BURIAL CHAMBER
DATE: mid-Neolithic and Early Bronze Age
MAP REF.: 818544
DIRECTIONS: 1-inch O.S. map. The track
past the farm to the site is signposted at the road.
Guide, price 4*d*, from the farm, entry free.

In 1924 the cromlech was in such a parlous con-
dition, with trees growing out of it, that the
Ministry of Works decided to put it in order and
excavate it at the same time, though not very ex-
tensively. Before this, in 1853, one chamber was
rescued from use as a stable, and the two others
and passage were discovered and cleared. The
line of a wall fencing the inner cairn is marked out
with white stones, but the restored cairn has been
kept low enough to show the chambers, only one

now roofed with the original large capstone, and passage into them, while covering the forecourt floor. All of this was originally covered completely by the outer mound. The skilful building of the dumbbell-shaped chamber can be seen restored to its original state, with gaps between the megaliths filled with dry-stone walling. The entrance was along the passage from the long side of the cairn, the only part that was thoroughly excavated in 1924. Here were found a fragment of western neolithic (A) pottery, near it a small flint flake struck by human hand, and pieces of two beakers. The passage was roofed by corbelling, the whole wall sloping inwards from the ground. The forecourt in the east end did not give on to an entrance. This is a common enough feature in south-east Wales among the Cotswold-Severn long barrows. It was scattered with white quartz, and was no doubt the scene of important ceremonies before it was carefully filled in with stones and covered over with the outer cairn. It is possible that the blocking of the entrance passage was removed from time to time to allow of more burials. Fires had been lit in it, perhaps to propitiate the earlier inhabitants of the tomb. Professor Grimes, surely rightly, believes that the purpose of the dummy forecourt was 'to isolate the dead by deceiving dead and living alike as to the ways into and out of the tomb'.

Arch. Camb., 1927

MOEL FENLLI

HILL-FORT
DATE: first century B.C.–fourth century A.D.
MAP REF.: 163600
DIRECTIONS: 1-inch O.S. map

The southernmost of the Clwyd forts, with an enclosed area of 63 acres. The main defences with three banks are on the north and east. The inner bank turns in and the outer is thickened at the western angle for the earliest entrance. The south-eastern entrance is later. Circular hollows probably remain from dwellings. Fragments of white and red pottery, flint arrowheads, corroded iron and glass were found during an excavation in 1849. A heath fire in 1816 uncovered more than 1,500 Roman coins, mostly denarii between A.D. 307 and 360. Forty-three of them are now in the Chester Museum. As so often, a Bronze Age cairn is included within the fort.

Ellis Davies, *Prehistoric and Roman Remains of Denbighshire*, 1929

PARC Y MEIRCH, DINORBEN

HILL-FORT
DATE: Early Iron Age to post-Roman
NAT. GRID.: 968756
DIRECTIONS: 1-inch O.S. map

The ramparts enclose about 5 acres. There was a small entrance at the north, where the quarry is advancing. The main one is at the south-east, where the defences are strongest, since there is there no natural protection. Excavation on the south end showed six distinct phases of occupation, reflected in building or alteration of the ramparts, one before the ramparts were built at all, since hut floors, charcoal, etc, lie under the earliest walled banks. This walled rampart stood during two following stages, and over it in the next three stages the great sloping-fronted rampart was erected and twice rebuilt or enlarged. The inner face of the main rampart was terraced to make wall walks at three levels.

The last stage, which continued after the departure of the Romans, began at the end of the third century. On the north-east, near the rampart, many hut floors have been uncovered recently, some under the earlier rampart, some above its ruins, with early second-century relics dating the habitation. Pieces of human skull in front of a pre-Roman hut remind us of the Celtic practice of sticking up the heads of enemies and criminals on stakes.

All the huts are round, built on platforms between 15 and 30 feet diameter dug into the rock up-slope, and once levelled up upwards down-slope, though this half has generally now weathered away. Gullies for drainage are often seen round the side of the platform. There is often a hearth in the centre, and usually part of a saddle quern beside it, many animal bones, small scraps of pottery, charcoal. Among some huts are signs of iron or lead smelting. Sling stones and iron spear-heads are the most commonly found weapons. Deer hunting must have been important, for antler and deer bone was much used for harness, tool handles, buttons, furniture fittings, possibly even for a harp. The busiest time was during the fourth century. Most of the coins found at the southern end belong between 335 and 353, though on the north few such late ones have been found. A large house, in traditional round style, built at the northern end in the centre, could have housed a chieftain responsible for defending the coast against piratical raids during the absence of the imperial troops. Eighteen coins were found of late third and early fourth century, and the ox head (fig. 45), a bracelet and other signs of prosperity. Oblong buildings, defined by rows of post-holes, probably indicate that occupation continued in the fifth century.

B.B.C.S., 1958
Tr. of Denbighshire Historical Society, 1959
Ellis Davies, *Prehistoric and Roman Remains of Denbighshire*, 1929

PEN Y CORDDYN, ABERGELE

HILL-FORT
DATE: *c.* first century A.D.
GRID REF.: 915765
DIRECTIONS: 1-inch O.S. map

Thirty-seven acres are enclosed. The stone rampart makes what use it can of natural rock outcrop. Main defence is needed on north and north-west. The fort is divided by a double wall, one half possibly being used for herding cattle. There is no sign of huts, and finds excavated were few: animal bones, mainly ox, with sheep, goat, horse and pig, no deer, charcoal and pot boilers, sling stones, corroded iron, and a piece of Gaulish Samian ware of the first century A.D. The fort seems rather a refuge for times of emergency than a permanent habitation. The rampart, in places strengthened by an outer bank, and ditch, has a broad fighting platform protected by a parapet of stone. The north-east entrance, approached by a hollow track, has square guard chambers at the inner end of a long narrow passage. The north-west entrance has a long passage and single gate. The southern has a crooked passage and a single gate. A sally port on the east is entered by a track leading to a spring. The entrances and guardhouses seem to have been deliberately filled in, and there is no indication of later occupation than the first or second century.

Ellis Davies, *Prehistoric and Roman Remains of Denbighshire*, 1929
Arch. Camb., 1910

PONT NEWYDD

CAVE WITH PALAEOLITHIC REMAINS
DATE: *c.* 60000 B.C.
MAP REF.: 016711
DIRECTIONS: 1-inch O.S. map, marked Cave. The opening is above the road, just where it turns after crossing the bridge.

Excavation has cleared the cave for some way back into the cave, but much of it remains full of clay, in which no doubt more animal bones are em-

bedded, and perhaps more human remains. In 1962 the writer found a small flake of stone, humanly struck, in the clay clinging to the cave wall. Unfortunately the earlier excavator has put much of his tip just outside the entrance, where, as has been learnt in recent years, traces of human habitation are most likely to be preserved. The implements are now in the Museum of Archaeology and Ethnography, Downing Street, Cambridge.

Boyd-Dawkins, *Cave Hunting*, 1874
Ellis Davies, *Prehistoric and Roman Remains of Denbighshire*, 1929

FLINTSHIRE

FFYNNON BEUNO AND CAE GWYN

CAVES WITH PALAEOLITHIC REMAINS
DATE: 25000 B.C.
MAP REF.: 085725
DIRECTIONS: The caves are side by side, a short distance behind the well and farmhouse, once an inn, Ffynnon Beuno. The house is on the Bodfari-Tremerchion road, set back on the east side just north of the village marked Graig on the 1-inch O.S. map.

Ffynnon Beuno is the lower and more easterly of the two caves. The large entrance passage leads to a wider chamber; at the junction, under the crumbled fragments of limestone, was found a flint knife close to a rhinoceros jaw, and near large pieces of mammoth limb bones. To the left a narrower tunnel bends back to the cliff face. This, when excavated in 1885, was undisturbed, whereas the larger passage was used, understandably, as a cattle shed. In this narrower gallery were the fossilized droppings of hyenas and pleistocene animal bones, many of them gnawed, reached to the floor, having been disturbed by melt-waters. Some showed signs of human working, one was pierced with a hole. The main chamber has been enlarged by mining in historical times from a shaft above, at the right-hand far corner. Round to the right is a narrow cavern where, sealed under a floor of stalagmite 6 feet down, flint implements, charcoal, and bones were found, among them the early Solutrean lance-head, close to a mammoth tooth. The bones are in various museums, the flints are in the British Museum of Natural History, South Kensington.

Cae Gwyn lies 20 feet higher up the cliff, a little to the north-west of Ffynnon Beuno. It is a long narrow tunnel in which rhinoceros, lion, bear, reindeer and red deer bones were found, and a small well-made flint end-scraper. The main entrance is, in fact, at the far end, but until 1886 it was completely blocked by glacial deposits. It is here that Aurignacian man found shelter. A worked flint knife was found here, just outside the present walls of the cave, for the cliff has crumbled away under the ice and then the melting that followed his occupation. Sea-shells were also found beneath many feet of glacial clays and sands. They are the same shells as those found on Moel Tryfan in Snowdonia, and were scoured by glaciers from the bed of the Irish Sea, to be deposited high up on the mountains, then, of course, deep under ice. The two implements from Cae Gwyn are in the British Museum of Natural History. Animal bones are in Tremerchion School and in the B.M.N.H. The importance of Cae Gwyn is that the knife lying under 17 feet of glacial deposit proves that man was in the cave before the final advance of the ice. At Pont Newydd, and even at Ffynnon Beuno, it could be argued that later flooding had mixed up all the evidence.

GOP HILL

CAVES AND CAIRN (fig. 49)

DATE: caves possibly inhabited as early as late mesolithic times, during fourth millennium; both inhabited and used as a burial chamber by neolithic people, third millennium B.C. Cairn undated, probably Bronze Age.

MAP REF.: 087802

DIRECTIONS: 1-inch O.S. map. Turn off the road to Llanasa from the middle of Trelawnyd (Newmarket). There is a footpath starting just beyond the new housing estate.

The rock shelter and cave behind it were excavated in 1886. Bones of cave hyena, bison, stag, reindeer, horse, roedeer and woolly rhinoceros lay in a pleistocene level near the bottom. Above this was a neolithic B occupation floor, with a fireplace covered with charcoal. Burnt stones and burnt animal bones and charcoal lay scattered about, and fragments of pottery. The small amount of this which has been preserved is neolithic B, and is in the Manchester Museum. Human bones also lay mixed with pottery and burnt animal bones under slabs of limestone reaching to the roof. Besides this was a square chamber built of regular courses of limestone, in which was a mass of human skeletons, tightly crouched and packed in, both

long and short-headed types. Among them a polished flint knife, white quartz pebbles and two long narrow pieces of polished shale with a large oval hole in the centre. These are thought to be belt fasteners and are known from other neolithic B burials. Sheep bones were common, no ox. Microliths were found scattered in front of the shelter.

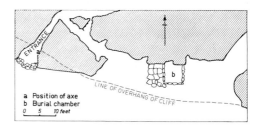

a Position of axe
b Burial chamber
0 5 10 feet

Fig. 49 *Plan of Gop Caves (After Ellis Davies 'Prehistoric and Roman Denbighshire')*

The north-west cave was discovered and excavated in 1908-14. The narrow passage was discovered leading to the cave, and its entrance from the cliff face which had been walled up in prehistoric times. Burials were found, some at least protected by walls of stone, in all the passages. Mussel shells were found, and a few animal bones, but no charcoal or pottery. Animal bones included ox, sheep, deer, bear, wolf, fowl and the only specimen known in Wales of a lynx. A perfect, unused and unpolished axe had been buried upright at the entrance. Microliths were found scattered in the cave earth. The skulls in this cave were all long-headed, all the bones were in fragments, but they belonged to small slender people, like those buried in caves at Cefn and Perthi Chwarau. A recent excavation has uncovered a new chamber (not in plan) with more neolithic burials.

It is impossible to say whether the microliths belong to earlier mesolithic occupation of the caves or were made by the neolithic inhabitants.

A shaft was sunk to the ground through the cairn in 1886, but nothing was found. This does not necessarily mean there is no chamber inside it, though it may have been raised to stand over the cave burials.

Arch. Camb., 1935
Ellis Davies, *Prehistoric and Roman Remains of Flintshire*, 1949

MOEL HIRADDUG, MOEL Y GAER, PEN Y CLODDIAU, MOEL ARTHUR, RHOSESMOR

HILL-FORTS
DATE: *c.* 350 B.C.–*c.* A.D. 400
GRID REF.: Moel Hiraddug, 064783; Moel y Gaer, 095709; Pen y Cloddiau, 130675; Moel Arthur, 145660; Moel y Gaer Caerfallwch, 201690
DIRECTIONS: 1-inch O.S. map

Moel Hiraddug is mainly defended on the east, its weakest side. Main entrance is at south-east, where each of the three ramparts has an incurved opening, some distance to the east of the outer defence. Another entrance at north-west. The shield was found when a modern entrance was made to reach the cobalt mine and iron quarry at the north-east. A few stone hut circles can be seen. The wide spacing of the ramparts links this fort with Dinas Bran, Llangollen, and with camps down the Marches and in Somerset, South Wales, Devon and Cornwall. There have been no Roman-period finds but only rough pottery, iron, bone and antler work from Iron Age occupation. One saddle quern lay in a hut, and a bronze pin of Late Halstatt type (300–210 B.C.) was found (see p. 52). Pen y Cloddiau has not been excavated. It is one of the largest forts in North Wales, more than 50 acres. It is defended with an earth rampart dug from an inner ditch. On the west side is a second rampart with inner ditch. The weakest natural side, on the north-west, has four ramparts. Entrances on south and east sides, inturned. Moel y Gaer, Bodfari, has no rampart on the steep east side; the rest has two ramparts, with inner ditches. Moel Arthur has a double rampart with outer ditches on the north, entrances on north-east and north-west; the rest of the 5 acres is defended by an artificial terrace, without a bank. Pits inside may be huts. Coarse Roman pottery, flint arrow-heads and rusty iron were excavated in 1849, and parts of a stone wall were uncovered near the rampart south of the north-west entrance. The hoard of Early Bronze Age flat axes was found towards the southern end of the fort. At Rhosesmor (Caerfallwch) the camp commands a wide view. There is a tumulus inside the fort. To the north the rampart is 20 feet above the ditch. In places there is a second rampart. Entrance to south-east. A bone piercer was found inside the camp.

R.C.A.M. Flintshire
Ellis Davies, *Prehistoric and Roman Remains of Flintshire*, 1949

PENBEDW PARK

STONE CIRCLE AND TUMULUS
DATE: Bronze Age
GRID REF.: 171679
DIRECTIONS: 1-inch O.S. map. Permission must first be sought from the owner, at Penbedw House.

Five of the eleven standing stones remain. Trees have stood for many years in the places of the lost stones. An outlier stands 244 paces to the west, 5 feet 4 inches high and 16 feet circumference. Nearer the house, and to the north, is a tumulus, in which in 1860 some food-vessel fragments and charcoal were found among 'large stones'.

Ellis Davies, *Prehistoric and Roman Remains of Flintshire*, 1949

MERIONETHSHIRE

CAER DREWYN

HILL-FORT
DATE: Iron Age
GRID REF.: 087445
DIRECTIONS: 1-inch O.S. map

This eight-acre fort lies on a spur 400 feet above the Dee. It is overtopped by higher ground to the east, but is well fortified there with outworks of rampart and ditch round the entrance. A stone-built rampart surrounds the site, but no ditch. There is an inturned entrance on the west, with small circular chambers in the walls. Traces of stone hut circles, probably later than the building of the fort, can be seen in the outworks, but not in the fort itself.

R.C.A.M. Mer.
Arch. Camb., 1926

CAER EUNI

HILL-FORT
DATE: Iron Age
GRID REF.: 000414
DIRECTIONS: 1-inch O.S. map. Leave the side road at Cwm Cottage and follow the track to the shoulder of the hill. Follow the field wall to the fort.

The stone rampart is badly robbed. A wide ditch with outer bank surrounds it a little distance down the slope all round. There is a cairn at about the centre, and an ancient bank runs across the middle. The fort dominates the valley to the south and the wide moorland, which has a number of burial cairns on it, to the north. The course of a Roman road, joining Ffridd and Caer Gai, runs along the south-east flank of the hill, but does not appear to have any direct communication with the camp. The forts it most closely resembles are Llandinam and Middletown in Montgomery.

Arch. Camb., 1926
R.C.A.M. Mer.

CARNEDDAU HENGWM, AND PEN Y DINAS

LONG-CHAMBERED CAIRNS, HILL-FORT, BOILING MOUND

DATE: *c.* 2500 B.C.; hill-fort, Iron Age

MAP REF.: Carneddau, 614205; hill-fort, 606208; boiling mound, 609208

DIRECTIONS: 1-inch O.S. map. Follow the track past the farm at Egryn Abbey and up the steep hill, until the cables of the disused manganese-mine railway can be followed to their terminus. From here looking eastward across the moor the two cairns are easy to see. The boiling mound is near the stream. Pen y Dinas is across the steep gully and is best reached by continuing eastwards from the Carneddau to join the track that comes down to Hengwm past the hill-fort. The circles marked on the map are now wellnigh invisible.

The southern carnedd is 190 feet long and 70 broad, lying east-west. The eastern chamber, beyond the modern wall, was a tall portal dolmen. The capstone has fallen. The western is built of masonry with a large capstone, and approached by a short passage from the north. The northern carnedd is smaller, 110 by 60 feet, also lying east-west. The eastern chamber is unclear, and may have been several together. In the centre is one similar to that in the centre of the southern carnedd, but without a passage. At the west end a large capstone lies on the top of some large standing stones. The track runs from a little farther east straight to the Cors y Gedol cromlech and on to the ruins at Bron y Foel. The highland here bears traces of continuous occupation, with the site of the Beaker or neolithic B circles north-east of Pen y Dinas, Bronze Age cairns along the track and on the hill-tops, and the Iron Age hill-fort. Two bridle bits of Iron Age B type were found near the coast at Llanaber.

The hill-fort has an inner circular rampart of earth held between two retaining walls of masonry. On the north and west there is a second rampart, faced with large boulders on the outside. The deep ditch between the two ramparts continues all round outside the inner rampart; there is a second outer ditch on the west, and traces of a third line of defence. There seem to be rough stone hut foundations outside the defences on the north. The defences recall those of Celtic La Tène *oppida* in France and Somerset of the fourth and third centuries B.C., and the bits corroborate this. Excavations of the fort revealed nothing for dating.

Arch. Camb., 1920
R.C.A.M. Mer.

CORS Y GEDOL

CROMLECH AND HUT CIRCLES IN FIELDS

DATE: early third millennium B.C. and early second century A.D.

MAP REF.: 602228

DIRECTIONS: 1-inch O.S. map, marked burial chamber (remains). The hut circles and field walls are on the ffridd to the east of the cromlech, in an area about 500 by 700 yards, with the cromlech in the middle of the western side.

The cromlech lies at the east end of a long low mound of earth and stones; its shape is now difficult to define. The capstone now leans from the top of one large stone to the ground, but probably originally was supported all round by standing stones, and protruded over a forecourt. The huts and fields are of several periods, terraces and walls dividing fields of many shapes and sizes. A path can be traced between them running from south-west to north-east. A hut group was excavated in 1956. It lies near the junction of the track leading to the cromlech with that running east from Cors y Gedol mansion. Three huts, two round and one rectangular, were built with an unusually flimsy enclosing wall round them. Walls 4 to 7 feet thick were of earth and small stones faced with massive stones. There was a drain running to a sump in one hut, and traces of a paved floor. A single post-hole with packing-stones may have been part of a ring of posts half-way between the wall and the centre to support a roof, probably of branches holding up turf. A pit held charcoal of willow and hazel and the remains of an oak bowl.

Pottery in the huts was of three kinds, fine black, rough hardware suitable for storage jars, and fine hard pink. This would date the occupation of these huts to early in the second century, in the time of Hadrian and just after. Slate disks, about an inch across, were also found, similar to disks found in other hut groups in Caernarfonshire and Anglesey. Their use is unknown.

J. Mer. H. and R. S., 1956
B.B.C.S., November 1958

CEFNDWYSARN

EARTHWORK
DATE: Iron Age
GRID REF.: 968382
DIRECTIONS: 1-inch O.S. map. A field gate from the side road to Llandderfel, at the top of the hill outside Cefndwysarn, leads up to the earthwork.

A fine ditch and rampart surround an oval area on the slope of the hill. This is obviously not built for defence, and may have been used for herding cattle. Similar sites are known in Cornwall, and a few others in Wales.

DYFFRYN LLANBEDR, GWERN EINION

CROMLECHAU
DATE: 3000 B.C.
GRID REF.: 589229, 588286
DIRECTIONS: Behind the school in Dyffryn.

At Dyffryn the excavation trenches and boundaries of the small oval and large rectangular cairns are marked with large stones. The western chamber has a natural slab as a floor. The eastern chamber had a socket dug for a movable upright to block the gap between the cross slab at the entrance and the southern orthostat. The blocking of the forecourt was very elaborate. Inside the chamber was one Beaker sherd, perforated rim fragments of late neolithic ware, and fragments of a Food Vessel lying below a small deposit of cremated bones.

Antiq., March 1963

Farther towards Harlech along the coast road is a stone with a spiral, probably from a cromlech, now in Llanbedr church, and in Llanbedr one turns off towards Gwern Einion for the cromlech now used as a cattle shelter.

LLANDRILLO: TYFOS CIRCLE; BRANAS BARROW; RHYD Y GLAFAIS CHAMBER

MEGALITHIC REMAINS IN THE DEE VALLEY
DATE: Late Neolithic-Early Bronze Age; *c*. 1600 B.C.
GRID REF.: 028388, 011375, 047397
DIRECTIONS: Tyfos circle: 1-inch O.S. map. In the field in front of the farmhouse. Branas: can be seen from the road, about half a mile to the east, after it leaves the railway. It is two fields westward away from the track running over the railway bridge to Branas Uchaf house. Rhyd y Glafais: a turning through a field gate just west

of the Rhyd y Glafais entrance. The lane swings round and through the ruined part of the cairn to the ruins of a farmhouse, to the north of the road. Tyfos circle is the kerb of a very large burial mound. A ring of fourteen boulders several feet apart stands a little within the circumference of the mound, which is still about 3 feet high. The mound at Branas is up to 8 feet high. Two large stones stand upright, one 5 feet above the mound. At Rhyd y Glafais the capstone, nearly 12 feet long, is uncovered. A passage leads from the lane, cutting through the cairn into the chamber, but its walling is modern. In the near corner of the next field, to the north-north-west, is a rise which may be a round barrow, nearly ploughed out.

R.C.A.M., Mer.

LLANDRILLO: MOEL TY UCHAF

STONE CIRCLE AND CAIRN
DATE: 1400 B.C.
GRID REF.: 056372
DIRECTIONS: 1-inch O.S. map. Straight up the lane at Caer Bont. Once on the moorland the old Ffordd Gam Elen curves round the base of the hill. The circle is hidden by the shoulder of the hill, but can be seen, with its outlier, as soon as the climb is done.

Remains of a cist lie near the centre. The stones are close set, without a visible bank, with an entrance at south-south-west. The diameter is 39 feet. At the foot of the hill to the south are the remains of a large circular cairn, diameter about sixty feet, with many blocks of white quartz, and possibly several other tumuli. The track passes a number of cairns on its way over to Llanrhaiadr ym Mochnant, where its descent into the Tanat valley is marked by two standing stones.

R.C.A.M. Mer.

MOEL GOEDOG AND OLD TRACKWAY

STONE CIRCLES, STANDING STONES AND HILL-FORT
DATE: Circles, *c*. 1300 B.C.; hill-fort, *c*. 100 B.C.; trackway, began *c*. 1600 B.C.
GRID REF.: 614325, 648358, 648353
DIRECTIONS: 1-inch O.S. map. The mountain track leaving the Eisingrug-Harlech upland road is well marked by standing stones. It passes close by the circles before it skirts the hill crowned by the fort.

The left-hand circle, first met with, is possibly a hut foundation, with a porch entrance, but the plan is not clear. A little farther on, on the right, is a perfect cairn circle. The track continues past hut circles and cairns across the hill-side and down past Cwm Moch to Maen Llwyd south of Traws-fynydd. There are hut circles near Eisingrug at 625344, close by the track at 643346, and again at 647357. Bryn Cader Faner (fig. 29), marked on the map, is a striking cairn circle, with tall orthostats held in a stone wall. Down towards Coetty Mawr from here one of the 'cairn circles' on the map is a very good example of a boat-shaped cist (fig. 28). At Maes y Caerau is a well-preserved cattle-farm site with three concentric rings. The fort on Moel Goedog has massive earth ramparts in Iron Age B tradition, and is divided by a line of outcrop across the middle.

R.C.A.M. Mer.

MURIAU'R GWYDDELOD, LLANDANWG

HUT CIRCLE
DATE: first century B.C. or Roman period
GRID REF.: 583303
DIRECTIONS: Climb the hill behind Harlech and take the footpath to the right running parallel with the coast. A brambly stretch full of ancient field boundaries is passed, then turn left up the hill and the great ring of stones is soon found.

A few rooms can be seen in the thickness of the wall. Other enclosed and unenclosed hut groups lie nearby on the hill-side.

R.C.A.M., Mer.

TOMEN Y MUR

ROMAN CAMP
DATE: A.D. 78–140
GRID REF.: 707388
DIRECTIONS: 1-inch O.S. map.

The first, 4-acre fort was built immediately after the defeat of the Ordovices by Agricola in the late summer of A.D. 78. Timber buildings were erected inside a turf and clay rampart which bore a wooden palisade, and a ditch. Later, about A.D. 110, the fort was rebuilt, with a smaller area. The north-west rampart was pulled down to allow a clear view from the new north-west wall which ran where now the medieval motte stands, using the reduced fort as its bailey and completely covering the Roman gateway. The timber buildings and palisade in the eliminated section were burnt, either by enemy action or by the builders; charred wood and ash lie under the unburnt levelled clay from the earlier rampart. Pottery finds show that the fort was occupied until about A.D. 140 or a little later.

The hollow by the road to the north-east of the fort is said to have been an amphitheatre, an unusual addition to so small a fort. Its size make it more likely a cockpit. Perhaps the bleakness of the surrounding country made it necessary to entertain the soldiers. There is a parade ground lying north-east of the fort, with a rectangular bank round it, all now rather marshy. Field boundaries show to the east and north-west. A road led away from the south-east gate south-eastwards past practice camps at Dolddinas and away to Caer Gai. Unevennesses in the ground along the road outside the fort show where a village grew up to serve the fort; a hypocaust (foundations for central heating) and other building was excavated in the area in the middle of the last century.

Eight stones inscribed with the number of yards built by the cohort of Julius Perpetuus were found during excavation, some querns, and pottery frag-ments. Four miles to the south at Pen Ystryd on the road to Dolgellau and Pennal was a small Roman tile works, which had three or more kilns; it made roof and floor tiles and domestic pottery between A.D. 80 and 150. Copper-mines farther down the valley on the east side were possibly worked at this time.

J. Mer. H. and R. S., 1962

MONTGOMERY

CRAIG RHIWARTH AND RHOS Y BEDDAU

HUT SETTLEMENT, AND AVENUE AND ARRANGEMENT OF STANDING STONES
DATE: Iron Age or Roman period; and probably Bronze Age
MAP REF.: 056271, 057301
DIRECTIONS: Best approached up Cwm Orog, where a path runs up the valley along the old mine rope railway. At the top cut up to the right over the crest, and the circles of hut foundations will be found spread widely over the summit. For keen walkers, 2 miles across the moorland from here almost due north is the site of the Rhos y Beddau avenue and semicircle. The 'cairn' marked on the map, in Cwm Rhiwiau, lies 144 feet north-north-east of the beginning of the avenue. This is difficult to find among the heather and bracken, but once found, it leads in 188 feet to the semi-circle with a standing stone beyond.

R.C.A.M., Mont.

Museums

The National Museum of Wales at Cardiff, of course contains the largest and most important collection of Welsh antiquities, and gives the fullest illustration of the prehistory of Wales, with finds from many important sites. Some cases are arranged to demonstrate the development of tools and weapons, and the display is supplemented with maps, diagrams and explanatory notices and labels.

The *University Museum* at Bangor has a room devoted to North Welsh antiquities which is full of interesting material. *Grosvenor Museum*, Chester, includes a number of finds from North Wales, particularly pots and bronzes of interest, mostly of the Bronze Age; it also contains many interesting Roman exhibits. Nineteenth-century finds from North Wales are mostly in the *British Museum* in London. Apart from the unique gold ornaments (of which there are perfect copies at Cardiff) and the Moel Siabod shield, most objects are not on display, but they can be seen on request, if notice is given. The Museum on the site of *Segontium*, at Caernarfon, contains all the material from excavations there, and other local finds.

Reading List

Reports of discoveries and excavations are published yearly in the following periodicals, and the back numbers contain all the information on which any prehistory of the region is based.

Archaeologia Cambrensis (*Arch. Camb.*).
Bulletin of the Board of Celtic Studies (*B.B.C.S.*).
The Transactions of the Archaeological, Historical or Field Society of each county.
A Bibliography of the History of Wales, 1962, published by University of Wales gives all references (in Section C).

The following are also recommended for further reading. Some, written before the use of Carbon 14 dating, may be out of date in details, but still contain the essential information:

The Inventories of the Royal Commission of Ancient and Historical Monuments in Wales and Monmouthshire:

Anglesey, 1937 (R.C.A.M. Anglesey).
Caernarvonshire I (East), 1956 (R.C.A.M. Caern. I).
Caernarvonshire II (Central), 1960 (R.C.A.M. Caern. II).
Caernarvonshire III (West), 1964 (R.C.A.M. Caern. III).
Denbighshire, 1914 (R.C.A.M. Denb.).
Flintshire, 1912 (R.C.A.M. Flints.).
Merionethshire, 1921 (R.C.A.M. Mer.).
Montgomeryshire, 1911 (R.C.A.M. Mont.).
Ellis Davies, *Prehistoric and Roman Remains of Denbighshire*, 1929.
Ellis Davies, *Prehistoric and Roman Remains of Flintshire*, 1949.
These two books supplement the very out-of-date R.C.A.M. Inventories with much detail.
W. F. Grimes, *The Prehistory of Wales*, 1951. Guide and Catalogue to the Prehistoric Collection of the National Museum of Wales.
R. E. M. Wheeler, *Prehistoric and Roman Wales*, 1925. Still the only general account.
S. Piggott, *British Prehistory*, 1949. A useful general introduction.
G. Daniel, *Prehistoric Chamber Tombs of England and Wales*, 1950.
Sir Cyril Fox, *The Personality of Britain*, 1952. With many distribution maps, and emphasis on Wales.
W. F. Grimes, The Megalithic Monuments of Wales (*Proceedings of the Prehistoric Society*, 1936). A comprehensive field survey.
S. Piggott, *Neolithic Cultures of the British Isles*, 1954.
Sir Cyril Fox, *Life and Death in the Bronze Age*. A study of burials and burial rites.
I. A. Richmond, *Roman Britain*, Pelican, 1963.
W. Gardner, 'The Native Hillforts in North Wales', *Arch. Camb.*, 1926. A field survey with plans.
V. E. Nash-Williams, *The Roman Frontier in Wales*, 1954.
Sir Cyril Fox, *A Find from the Early Iron Age at Llyn Cerrig Bach*, 1945.
H. N. Savory, The Tal y Llyn hoard, *Antiquity*, March 1964.

Maps

Ordnance Survey 1-inch maps of the area.
Ordnance Survey $\frac{1}{4}$-inch maps of the area.
Ordnance Survey, The Map of Southern Britain in the Iron Age includes valuable introduction summarizing the Iron Age in Britain.
Ordnance Survey, The Map of Roman Britain.
Ordnance Survey, Ancient Britain, southern sheet.

Index

Aberdaron, Caernarvon 14
Aberffraw, Anglesey 15, 44, 68
Abergele, Denbigh. 68
Aberystwyth, Card. 14, 15
Afon Lliw, Merioneth. 48
Agriculture 28, 53, 58, 59, 60, 70, 71
  72
Altars, Roman 69, 70
Animals in Celtic art 63, fig. 45, 64
Ardudwy, Caern. 72
Arthog, Merioneth. 48
Aurignacian implements fig. 3, 13
Avebury, Wiltshire 32, 46

Bala, Merioneth. 30
Bala Lake, Merioneth. 36, fig. 30, 48
Bangor, Caern. 36
Barclodiad y Gawres, Anglesey 20, 22
Bath-houses, Roman 67, 68, 69, 70
Beads
  Amber 39, fig. 26, 51
  Faience 43
  Glass 71
  Jet 39
  Pottery 43
  Roman 70
Beaker people 27–30, 34
Beakers, 28, fig. 11, 29, 30
Beddgelert, Caern. 36, 49
Belgae, The 53
Belt fastener, jet 24
Boiling mounds 41–42, 49
Bone
  necklace 27
  pin fig. 6, 18
  pendant 27
Bowls
  Bronze 54–55, fig. 39
  Pottery 23
  Wood 52–53, fig. 37, 71
Bracelets 39, 70
Braich y Dinas, Caern. 70, 71
Bronze Age 31–46
Bronze implements
  Axe-hammers 49
  Axes 32, fig. 16, 33, 35, 37, fig. 21,
    39, 51
  Bowls 54, fig. 39, 55
  Chisels fig. 16, 39, fig. 26, 46
  Daggers fig. 16, 33, 36, 49
  Halberds 33, 47

Harness fittings 39, fig. 26, 50, 58
Hoards 38, 39, 62
Knives 11, 39, 45
Moulds for 33, fig. 17, 36, 39, 48, 49
Palstaves fig. 17, 36, fig. 20, 39, 41,
  46, 47, 48, 49
Personal objects 39, fig. 26, 42, 48,
  50
Rapiers 36, 48
Sickles 48, fig. 31, 49
Smith's hoard 39, fig. 25
Spearheads 36, fig. 22, 39, fig. 25,
  47, 48, 49
Swords 37, fig. 25, 49, fig. 33, 56
Brooches 70, 71
Bryllysg, Merioneth. 58
Brymbo, Denbigh. 29
Bryn Celli Ddu, Anglesey 20, 22,
  fig. 8, 23, 24
Brynford Mountain 58
Bryn Gwyn, Anglesey 27
Bryn Llwyn, Flints. 27
Bryn y Gefeiliau, Anglesey 66, 67
Bryn yr Ellyllon, Flints. 51
Bryn yr Hen Bobl, Anglesey 18, 19,
  23, 24, 25
Brynkir, Caern. 49
Buckets, bronze 38, fig. 23, 48, 54
Burials
  Barrows see Tumuli
  Cairns 19, 20, 29, 34, 35, 43, 46, 49
  Cemeteries 29, 35
  Chamber tombs 22
  Cists 29, fig. 14, 43, 44, 45, 47, fig.
    28, 49, 54, 64
  Cromlechau 16, 17, fig. 5, 18, 19,
    20, 22, 23, 29, 34
  Passage graves 20, 34
  Tumuli 19–21, 29, 34, 35, 42, 44,
    49, 50, 51
Buttons, jet fig. 11, 29, 43
Bwlch y Ddeufaen, Caern. 50, 66
Bwlch y Gwrhyd, Caerhun, Caern. 29
Bwlch y Maen, Caern. 33

Cae Gwyn cave, Flint. fig. 3, 13, 15
Cae Mickney, Anglesey 35
Caerau, Caern. 59
Caer Dwreyn, Merioneth. 58, 70, 71
Caer Engan, Caern. 56
Caer Euni, Merioneth. 58

Caer Gai, Merioneth. 66, 67
Caergwrle Castle, Flints. 52
Caer Gybi, Anglesey 72
Caerhun, Caern. 69
Caer Leb, Anglesey 71
Caer Lleion on Conwy, Caern. 55, 56,
  59
Caernarvon 59, 66, 67, 68, 69, 70, 72
Caerwent, Mont. 65
Caerwys, Flints. 51
Caer y Twr, Anglesey 70, 71
Cairn circles 45, 46, 48
Capel Garmon, Denbigh. 20, 29, 64
Carbon 14: 10, 42
Carn Boduan, Caern. 55, 56, 59
Carn Fadrun, Caern. 55, 56
Carneddau Hengwm, Merioneth. 19,
  34
Castell Mawr, Llangelynin 58
Castell Odo, near Aberdaron, Caern.
  54, 58
Cefn, Denbigh. 19
Cefn Golau, Flint. 43
Celtic culture fig. 38, fig. 39, 55,
  fig. 40, 60, 63, fig. 45, 64, fig. 46
Cerrig y Drudion, Denbigh. 54, fig.
  39, 55
Chariots and chariot fittings 61, fig.
  44, 62, 63
Clegyr Boia, Pemb. 16
Clocaenog forest 44, 50, 58
Clwyd valley, Denbigh. 11, 19, 20, 58
Clynnog, Caern. 49
Coins and coin-hoards 68, 69, 70, 71
Conwy, River 58
Copper implements
  Axes 31
  Daggers 29
  Halberds 47
Copper-mines 53, 68
Cornovii, The 60
Cors y Gedol, Merioneth. 71
Corwen, Merioneth. 31, 50
Craig Rhiwarth, Mont. 68
Craig y Dinas, Llanaber, Merioneth.
  58
Craig y Dinas at Llanddwywe,
  Merioneth. 58
Craig y Dinas on Llyn, Caern. 55, 56,
  58
Cremation rite 23, 27, 34, 35, 43, 45

Cresswell Crag cave, Derby. 12, 13, 14
Cwm Moch, near Maentwrog, Merioneth. 36, 48
Cynwyd, Merioneth. 50

Danesfield, Bangor, Caern. 49
Darowen, Mont. 29, 45, 47
Deceangli, The 58, 60, 65
Derwen Moor 58
Disgwylfa Fawr, Mont. 46
Dinas, Caern. 24
Dinas Dinlle, Caern. 56, 70
Dinas Emrys, Caern. 72
Din Dryfol, Anglesey 20
Dinllaen, Caern. 56
Din Llugwy, Anglesey 71
Dinorben, Denbigh. 39, 50, 54, 55, 58, 64, 71
Dinorwig, Caern. 55, 56, 60, 67, 71
Din Silwy, Anglesey 70
Dolgellau, Merioneth. 30, 47
Druidism 34, 44, 45, 46, 49, 60–61
Dyffryn Ardudwy, Merioneth 16, fig. 4, 17, fig. 5, 19, 25, 29, 34
Dyserth, Flint. 19, 25, 27

Eglwyseg Mountain 50

Ffridd y Garreg Wen, Flint. 45
Ffridd, Merioneth. 67
Ffynnon Beuno, Flint. fig. 3, 13, 15
Fire-dogs 64, fig. 46
Forts 53, 55, 56, 58, 59, 66, 68, 69, 70, 71, 72
Fynnon Beuno cave, Flint. 13, 15

Garreg Fawr, Caern. 24
Glaciations 9–11
Gloddaeth, near Colwyn Bay, Caern. 36
Glyn, Anglesey 19
Goldsmiths' work 33, 41, 47, 48, 49, fig. 34, 51, fig. 36
Gop Cairn, Flint. 51
Gop Cave, Flint. 14, 15, 19, 24
Graig Lwyd, Penmaenmawr, Caern. 21, 24, 26, fig. 10
Great Orme, Caern. 46, 53, 68
Guilsfield, Mont. 39
Gwaenysgor, Flint. 25, 26, 27, 67
Gwern Einion, Merioneth. 48

Halkyn Mountain 68
Halstatt culture 52–53, 54
Harlech, Merioneth. 48
Hen Drefor, Anglesey 20
Hiraethog, Denbigh. 50
Holt, Denbigh. 66, 67

Homo sapiens 12
Horseshoes 71
Huts
    Stone 56, 58, 60, fig. 43, 70, 71
    Wooden or daub and wattle 58–59

Inscriptions, Roman 65, 66, 69
Iron Age A culture 53, 54
Iron Age B culture 53, 56
Iron Age C culture 53, 61
Iron Age hoard 61

Kanovium *see* Caerhun

La Tène culture 52–53, 54
Lead 65, 68
Leather craft 53
Llanasa, Flint. 27
Llanaelhaern, Caern. 59
Llanbabo, Anglesey 43
Llanbedr, Caern. 48
Llandecwyn, Merioneth. 44
Llandegai, Caern. 23
Llandrillo, Merioneth. 46
Llandudno, Caern. 68
Llandwrog, Caern. 70
Llanelltyd, Merioneth. 30, 47
Llanfachreth, Merioneth. 47
Llanfaethlu, Anglesey 69
Llanfairfechan, Caern. 69
Llangynog, Mont. 68
Llangwyllog, Anglesey 39, 51
Llanidan, Anglesey 70
Llanrhaiadr, Denbigh. 46, 48
Llanuwchllyn, Merioneth. 48, 49
Llecheiddior Uchaf, Caern. 49
Llechwedd Du, Merioneth. 69
Llithfaen, Caern. 29
Llong, Flint. 43
Llugwy, Anglesey 19, 23
Llyn, Caern. 19, 42, 48, 49, 54
Llyn Bugeilyn, Mont. 46
Llyn Cerrig Bach, Anglesey 61, 62, 63
Llyn Gwernan, Merioneth. 47

Mallwyd, Merioneth. 36
Marianbach, Cwn, Flint. 42
Meliden, Flint. 68
Menai Bridge, Anglesey 35
Menai Straits, Battle of 60
Merddyn Gwyn, Anglesey 29, 42, 45
Mesolithic period 13–15
Milestones, Roman 67, fig. 48
Moel Arthur, Denbigh. 51
Moel Fenlli, Denbigh. 58, 70, 71
Moel Goedog, Merioneth. 48, 58
Moel Hebog, Caern. 29
Moel Hiraddug, Flint. 54, 55, fig. 40, 56, 58
Moel Siabod, Caern. 49

Moel Ty Uchaf, Merioneth. 46
Moel yr Henblys, Mont. 47
Mold, Flint. 51
Mousterian 11, fig. 2, 13
Muriau'r Gwyddelod, Merioneth. 72
Mynydd Rhiw, Bryncroes, Llyn, Caern. 25, 26, fig. 10

Necklaces
    Amber 41
    Bone 27
    Gold-plated bronze 70
    Jet bead 42, 50
Neolithic village 27
Newborough Warren, Anglesey 14
Newydd Cave, Denbigh. 11

Ordovices, The 53, 59, 60, 65
Oyster shell disk fig. 3, 15

Pant y Saer, Anglesey 19, 25, 29
Parc y Merich, Dinorben, Denbigh. 39, 54, 58
Pared Llechymenyn, Caern. 14
Parys Mountain 68
Passage grave art fig. 7, 52
Paviland cave, Glam. 12, 14
Penbedw Park, Flint. 46, 50
Pencilan Head, Caern. 14
Pen Dinas, Card. 56–57
Pengarnedd, Anglesey 68
Penmaenmawr. Caern. 25, 34, 44, 45, 50
Penrhyndeudraeth, Merioneth. 49
Pentir, Caern. 69
Pentraeth, Anglesey 29
Pentre, Pemb. 51
Pen y Bonc, Anglesey 43
Pen y Corddyn, Denbigh. 58, 70, 71
Pen y Gaer, Llanbedr y Cennin, Caern. 56, 59
Pen y Gwryd, Caern. 67
Perthi Chwarau, Denbigh. 19, 24
Physical characteristics 29–30, 34
Pigmy cups 35, fig. 20, 47
Plas Penrhyn, Anglesey 35
Pont Newydd Cave, Denbigh. 11, fig. 2, 12
Pont Rhyd y Sarn, Card. 67
Porth Dafarch, near Pen y Bonc, Anglesey 43
Pottery
    Beaker 28, fig. 11, 34
    Bronze Age fig. 19, 42, 43
    Iron Age 54
    Roman 66, fig. 47, 67, 68, 70, 71
Prestatyn, Flint. 14, 15, 66, 68
Pumlumon, Mont. 30, 68

Querns 56, 58, 70, 71

Rhiwiau, Caern. 66, 67
Rhostryfan, Caern. 71
Rhuddlan, Flint. 66
Roads, Roman 66
Round houses 72
Ro Wen, Caern. 66

Saucepans, bronze 69
Segontium *see* Caernarvon
Selgovae, The 60
Sgethin Mountain 59
Shields 38, fig. 24, 47, 48, 49, 55,
    fig. 41, 56
Silures, The 53, 65
Sling near Bangor, Caern. 19
Spindle whorls 70
Stone circles 34, 44, 45, fig. 29, 46, 48,
    49, 53
Stonehenge, Wilts. 32, 34
Stone implements
    Adzes fig. 9, 24, 25
    Arrowheads fig. 6, 23, 25, 27, 31,
        fig. 14, 34, 46
    Awls 25
    Axes fig. 6, 23, 24, fig. 9, 25, 27, 43, 47
    Axe-hammers 48, fig. 32
    Boring tools 24
    Chisels 24

Choppers 25
Gravers fig. 3, 25
Hammer stones 24, 25, 27, 47
Hoes 23, 24
Knives 25, fig. 14, 34
Lance points fig. 3
Mace-heads 23, 27, 31, fig. 15, 43
Microliths fig. 3, 14, 15
Saws 25
Scrapers fig. 3, 24, 25
Stones, carved fig. 7, 22, 24, 48
Stones, standing 45, 47, 48, 49, 50

Talar Goch, Flint. 68
Talerddig, Mont. 46
Tal y Llyn, Anglesey 55, 62
Tanat, River 58
Tanat Valley fig. 30
Tankards 53, fig. 38, 54, 55, 64
Tan y Muriau, near Rhwiu, Caern. 19
Tomen y Mur, Llystyn, Merioneth.
    66, 67
Tonfannau, Merioneth. 47
Trackways 46–51, fig. 30
Trawsfynydd, Merioneth. 53, 55
Trearddur Farm, Anglesey 70
Tre' Castell Henryd, Caerhun, Caern.
    68

Trefignath, Holyhead, Anglesey 20
Tremadoc, Caern. 67, 68
Tre'r Ceiri, Caern. 56, fig. 57, 70, 71
Triskele ornament fig. 40, 55, fig. 41,
    56, 62
Tyddyn Bleiddyn, Cefn, Denbigh.
    19, 20
Ty Mawr, Holyhead, Anglesey 39
Ty Newydd, Anglesey 29
Ty'n y Pwll, Llanddyfnan, Anglesey
    34

Urns 34, fig. 18, 35, fig. 19, 42, 43, 47

Valley, Anglesey 61
Veneti, The 56
Votive hoards 61

Welshpool, Mont. 64
Wessex, position and influence of 32
Wood-carving 53
Wooden vessels 35

Y Foel, Caern. 56
Ynys Gwrtheyrn, Merioneth. 69
Ystrad Gwyn 62